THROWING UP

Notes from 35 Years of Juggling

By Leif Pettersen

Throwing Up: Notes from 35 Years of Juggling
Copyright © 2018 by Leif Pettersen

Visit the author's website at www.leifpettersen.com.

All rights reserved, including the right to reproduce this book or portions thereof in any form whatsoever.

Editor: Rachel Brougham

Cover Design: Renee Tanner

ISBN: 9781730712265

First Edition: November, 2018

Chapters

Acknowledgments..4

Glossary You Should Probably Read First....................6

Introduction..10

I Gatto Learn How to Juggle.......................................18

Coming of Age...40

Professional Show Off...54

MONDO – It Means Big...76

Juggling Is Easy – and Incredibly Difficult..................84

Let's Get Mental..96

Let's Get Physical.. 108

Go to Hell, David Hasselhoff.....................................128

By The Numbers..133

WTF Is Combat Juggling?..147

Why Juggling Is More Exciting Than All the Sports....156

How I Became A Competitive Athlete at Age 44..........163

Juggling, My Old Friend...191

Author Biography..199

Acknowledgments

Hello curious and attractive reader! Thank you for buying this book. You are the wind beneath my wings! (In this analogy, wind is money and wings is my savings account.)

Acknowledging everyone who played a significant role over the course of my 35 years of juggling isn't easy, even if I could remember every single person, which I definitely cannot. I'm going to do my best, though. If I forget someone important, I blame all the bell-ringing shots to the head by juggling clubs I've taken over the years.

Steve Birmingham, my Duck and Cover teammate and passing partner of more than 25 years, gets credit for his insatiable capacity for juggling, which has often reluctantly gotten me into the gym over the years when I'd much rather be watching TV. He also gets credit for coming up with some of our craziest tricks, which frequently put him in peril, to which I say better him than me. How he hasn't been permanently disfigured (yet) is the only sliver of doubt nagging my otherwise unwavering atheism.

The Minnesota Neverthriving Juggling Club, and its rotation of friendly, supportive, wildly talented members, are probably the only reason why my dalliances with juggling lasted more than a couple years. This wonderful cast of characters include the late Scott Burton, Keith Johnson (A.K.A. Jons The Juggler) and Jerry Martin, who were all there at day one.

Throwing Up – Acknowledgments

Special thanks goes to props-maker Brian Dubé who, upon hearing the rumor I was a vicious destroyer of clubs,[1] sent me prototype clubs for years, with instructions to break them and send them back, so he could perfect their durability.

Despite being weirdo unicyclists, I'm indebted to Constance and Andy Cotter, who let me crash their practice space and drink their alcohol for years.

Thank you to the mix of juggler and non-juggler manuscript readers, whose input helped make this book not suck for either audience: Ben Bowman, Annemarie Dooling, Mark Hayward, Brendan Kennealy Doug Mack, Pam Mandel, Katie Mardis, Lillie Marshal, Timothy Pate and Dave Walbridge.

Two people that literally helped make this book not suck are my editor Rachel Brougham and cover designer Renee Tanner. And a big thank you to my mom Linda Pettersen and girlfriend Liz Puhl, typo assassins of the first order.

Finally, I'm indebted to the generous early reviews and cover blurbs from Jay Gilligan and Dan Holzman.

---

[1] You break five brand new clubs in one week just *one* time and you're marked for life.

Glossary You Should Probably Read First

Like most any sport, activity, discipline or art, juggling has a glorious amount of bizarre terminology, much of which makes no sense, just like most things geeks produce. In order to soften the blow of non-jugglers' entry into this world, I have done my best to introduce new terminology in this book at a controlled rate, so it's not like the first season of "Game of Thrones," where you have to pause every four minutes to look up who's who and how soon their heads will be chopped off.

But in the unlikely event you put down this book, for whatever emergency, and pick it up weeks later having forgotten what a "multiplex" is, here's a glossary for quick reference.

First things first, you're gonna want to familiarize yourself with the key parts and details of a standard juggling club.

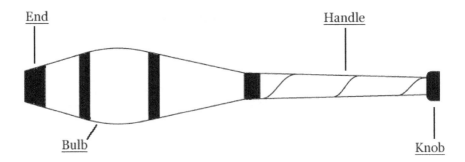

Juggling clubs come in many shapes and sizes. The ones we use (Henrys Delphin Long clubs) are about 20 inches long (52 centimeters) and a half pound in weight (0.2 kilograms). In addition to our preference for size and weight, Delphins have the added advantage of being remarkably durable. This is important, because even when we're in a good mood, we beat the hell out of those things.

Glossary

Cascade – A standard, crossing juggling pattern that looks and behaves a lot like a figure-8 car racing track, usually with odd-numbered objects, almost always the first pattern taught to novices.

Civilians – Non-jugglers.

Club passing – Two or more people throwing any number of clubs back and forth in rhythm, using predetermined timing.

Drop lines – Comments and jokes acknowledging a drop during a performance that fill time and entertain as the performer resets the trick.

Eat-the-apple – Both a popular juggling trick for civilians, entailing juggling two balls and an apple while consuming the apple, and unofficial shorthand for the kinds of lame tricks that non-jugglers believe are the pinnacle of juggling skill.

End bounce – When a juggling club is bounced off the floor with the thicker, padded end-side down (versus the knob side).

Flash – Usually employed while learning to juggle large numbers of objects, a "flash" is throwing all of the objects just once through the pattern, then stopping to revel in the amazingness of it all.

Flat bounce – When a juggling club is bounced off the floor length-wise.

Fountain – A juggling pattern that vaguely looks like a circle, often depicted in cartoons.

Hatchet throw – So named because it looks like someone making an overhand toss of a hatchet.

Helicopter spin – A juggling club spinning on a horizontal plane.

International Jugglers' Association – The chief global juggling body, which hosts annual festivals and world championship competitions in North America.

Juggle – As a noun, a "juggle" refers to successfully running all objects through a pattern two or more times. For three balls, this means at least six successful catches.

Multiplex – Throwing two or more objects from one hand simultaneously.

Numbers juggling – Generally speaking, this means juggling more than five objects.

Professional show off – A juggler.

Propeller spin – A juggling club spinning on a vertical plane.

Scissors catch – Using two clubs, gripped in such a way that they look like a giant pair of scissors, to catch a club and hold onto it by the knob.

Self-throw – A single throw to one's self, which doesn't include a trick or a pass to another person.

Shower – See "Fountain."

Static throw – A thrown club that has no rotation in any direction.

Steve's fault – Probably Leif's fault.

Stupid – Anything that Leif thinks is stupid or can't do, which is therefore stupid.

Introduction

"Three-Club Multiplex Hatchet" – Duration: 3.4 seconds

I am tense, because I know what's coming and it's not good, personal safety-wise.

Standing about 12 feet in front of me, wearing the neutral, but focused facial expression we've both accidentally cultivated over the years, my teammate Steve has gathered three juggling clubs[2] in his right hand and cocked his arm back over his head. Best case, what happens next is going to be stressful. Worst case is the all too familiar sound of wood thwacking bone, as one or more of my body parts takes a hit from a rapidly descending, spinning club handle. I wouldn't describe the sensation as pure terror; more like short-notice tragedy aversion.

The trick Steve is attempting, which we call a "three-club multiplex hatchet,"[3] is not one of his strengths. As is the case with most of our tricks, one of us is stronger at performing this trick than the other. Having shown more aptitude early on, and subsequently gotten in a lot more practice with it, Steve does not throw this trick at me in performance, or even most practices—I throw it at him. But once in a while for the sake of variety—but the pure joy of

---

[2] Also sometimes known as "pins," but never, no matter what, called "bowling pins," unless you want to sound like a total noob.
[3] A "hatchet throw" is so named because it looks like someone making an overhand toss of a hatchet.

screwing with me is always a possibility—he'll make a few attempts at this trick while we're warming up. This usually occurs with no warning, because that's how we operate.

I'm gonna pause for a second and break this moment down, with the accompanying torrent of emotions. Like a parent high-tossing a baseball so their kid can practice catching pop-ups, in the next fraction of a second Steve will hurl all three clubs in a high arc. But instead of a single, perfectly round object falling toward a cushioned baseball glove, three misshapen clubs, one side with a large screw slightly, but lethally, protruding out of it, will come pinwheeling down at my body/head/face. I'm going to catch these with my bare hands, at least that's the understanding, but there are caveats.

What's supposed to happen here is the three clubs should gently split away from each other in mid-air, forming into tall, thin triangle formation. The two low flying clubs will be caught first, simultaneously one in each hand, preferably by the handles, but we generally don't fuss over handles versus bottle catches.[4] The final club will be caught in whichever hand is closest to its descent—it can go either way—a fraction of a second after freeing said hand by tossing the club that's already occupying that space into a self-throw

---

[4] A bottle catch is when the club is caught on the bulb side, not the handle. This happens with Steve and I constantly and is no big deal. Others aren't as forgiving as we are and prefer that the club(s) are thrown correctly in the first place. We call these people "uppity." That said, clubs landing vertically, i.e. end or knob-side down, or any other angle, can be a problem.

or immediately dishing it back to the other person.[5] How to escape this bombardment of clubs without injury and, preferably, catching them all, is entirely up to the catcher. Since this trick is difficult and unpredictable, even when I'm throwing it, there's usually a fair bit of improvisation involved.[6]

However, since Steve is throwing this unfamiliar, highly volatile trick, there's a strong chance something will be wrong with the angle, speed, height, spin, position or any number of other micro-factors that plague jugglers with every single throw. This can result in the clubs landing short of my reach or behind me or on either side of me or just a buffet of missiles plummeting all around me. The latter is usually caused by a devastating mid-air collision, not uncommon when three clubs are spinning together in close proximity. If that happens, my default reaction is unashamed panic. Instead of trying to catch all the clubs, I'll do a kind of Matrix-style body slither around them to avoid injury. I might also throw in a high-pitched, faux-terrified yelp for theatrical purposes.

And we're back in the moment. As Steve heaves this whirling bundle of high-probability pain into the air, I have about 0.8 seconds from the time it leaves his hand to assess all three clubs and make a light-speed judgment about whether or not they're catchable based on their trajectory and spin.

---

[5] What I like to call a "Return to Sender" throw.
[6] Honestly, this can be said of nearly all our tricks.

If it's a go for catching, with the roughly 0.8 seconds I have left before indecision results in bodily harm (and a good story for Steve to tell people later), I need to devise and implement a plan to catch the two bottom clubs as they descend at what seems 120 mph. I'll worry about the top club later.

Assuming that catching the bottom pair of clubs goes well and relatively pain-free, it's time to get a final read on the top club, descending at 250 mph, and figure out where and how I'm going to catch it and where and how I'm going to get rid of one of the clubs in my hands to make that possible. Then, with whatever tenths of a second I have left before impact, I free the appointed hand and catch the final club.

In the event that things don't look orderly or safe, I have a few options. I can catch just one or two of the clubs, avoiding the rest with my finely tuned Agent Smith moves, or flee the scene entirely if Steve has totally biffed the throw.

It's best to completely remove oneself from situations like this, because, more often than you'd guess, one of the clubs will hit the ground in such a way that it immediately bounces back into the air with alarming force and height. This now weaponized club, obscured down in a total blind spot, usually flies harmlessly away. But sometimes, when the universe is feeling ornery, it will bounce straight up into one's produce section. This is followed by an indulgently long break from practice, while an adult man cries.

From start to finish, all these actions and the associated rollercoaster of emotions will have taken up just over three seconds of a one-hour practice session. Allowing for water breaks and picking up clubs after we (probably Steve) screw up, this scenario can play out over a wide variety of tricks upwards of 100 times in an hour.

I've voluntarily submitted to this Steve-assisted lunacy, on and off, for about 25 years. We've long been known as the juggling duo "Duck and Cover."[7] We're a bit of a novelty act. Our thing is six-club passing—two people throwing clubs back and forth in rhythm, using predetermined timing, enlivened by creative patterns and tricks. Some teams will work up to passing seven, eight, nine or more clubs during their act. More if they are a team of three people or larger. Steve and I differ from other teams in that we *only* pass six clubs. And the otherwise crucial rhythm and predetermined timing rules are open to mild, sometimes egregious disregard.

Instead, we endeavor to do six club passing tricks no one has seen before, pushing the boundaries of what's realistic and sane. We dream up and practice tricks that only masochists and the highly delusional would consider. Tricks

---

[7] Tagline: "It's not a name, it's a warning." There were an amusing few moments in the mid-90s when we entertained the idea of calling ourselves "LSD" ("Leif and Steve Disaster," or some other D-word that we immediately forgot), but I assume there was a non-man-child in earshot who talked us out of it.

where frequent injuries are inevitable. We are a danger to ourselves—and others. And we're kind of famous for it.

Harking back to the subject of launching three clubs at my face with no warning, I should add this is not done out of aggression,[8] it's just how we do things. Likewise, I almost never alert Steve about what trick I plan to throw or when. After all this time juggling together, this communication isn't necessary. We're like an old married couple, there are few genuine surprises left. I know what trick he's going to throw long before clubs are in the air—and the same is conversely true for Steve—based on where the clubs are in his hands, how many he's holding, where his arm swings prior to release, his stance, the look in his eye and the low-level Vulcan mind-meld we've developed over the years.

But more on that tricky relationship later.[9]

This book, geared for both jugglers and non-jugglers, is a semi-autobiographical, enlightening profile of the sport, art and act of juggling. How juggling is magic without illusion, seemingly immune to physics, and the innumerable, remarkable ways it affects one's life. After more than 35 years of juggling, I have gone through many evolutions, realizations and reinventions. I'll detail my time as a juggler starting way back in the summer of 1982, when I taught myself to juggle in my backyard, to my dalliances as a performer in the 90s, to the present, including that time

---

[8] Usually.
[9] "Tricky," get it? Like a juggling trick? I kill me.

when I belatedly dove into the fray of competitive juggling at the ripe old age of 44.[10]

I'll dish on mistakes I've made, victories, defeats, advice for new jugglers and people who can go right to hell.[11]

If you were hoping for a deep dive into the history of juggling itself, you should a) read this book anyway and give copies to friends and family for an entire year's worth of birthdays, then b) acquire the works of Karl-Heinz Ziethen and his colleagues, namely "4,000 Years of Juggling," "Juggling: The Art and Its Artists" and "Virtuosos of Juggling: From the Ming Dynasty to Cirque du Soleil."

I have taken on the daunting task of making juggling (and my life) sound interesting to non-jugglers, primarily because these experiences have never been presented in this manner before. There are personal memoirs from basketball players, singers, classical musicians, leaders, politicians, ultimate Frisbee players, people who went to the Olympics one time for curling, embroiderers and just about every other thing you can imagine. So, why not juggling, one of the most demanding mental and physical disciplines humans can engage in?

This profile is not about clowns, circus people[12] or any of the other incarnations of juggling that had not that long ago lowered its popular culture legitimacy to just a hair

---

[10] Almost twice the age of most other competitors.
[11] I'm talking about you, David Hasselhoff.
[12] Both of which already have memoirs, by the way.

above miming.[13] It's about a juggler who has made it a key component of his life and other jugglers, ranging from die-hard hobbyists to professional performers, wunderkinds to the old guard, nerds to, well, everyone else. I'll level with you, there are a lot of nerds.

My hope is that this book will finally beam a light on the aspects of this singular sport and lifestyle that almost never get highlighted, no matter how many jugglers make it onto "America's Got Talent," only to lose to a break dance team.

At the very least, my goal is that you will come around to my belief that juggling is, at its heart, endlessly rich and fascinating.

Leif Pettersen
Minneapolis, 2018

---

[13] Yes, there's a mime memoir, too. Well, it's more of a biography of Marcel Marceau by a lover, but see what I mean? Everyone has a memoir.

I Gatto Learn How to Juggle

"Three into Five" – Duration: 5.8 seconds
We've been doing this trick for 20 years, and it's so damn difficult and finicky that we *still* struggle with it some days.

I gather three consecutive incoming clubs in my right hand in a kind of triangle configuration. I'm going to throw these clubs at Steve as a three-club multiplex, like the three-club multiplex hatchet throw described in the previous chapter, but thrown underhand and far less prone to smashed thumbs and terrified yelps.

As I'm winding up to pass this to Steve, he quickly throws the two clubs he's still holding about three feet straight up as double spins.[14] Then I flick the three-club multiplex at Steve, which should form into a narrow, tall triangle in the air. The two bottom clubs in the triangle simultaneously rocket as single spins straight across into Steve's now empty hands. The top club in the triangle does a double spin as it arcs and descends down to Steve's right hand. The two clubs he threw to himself 0.7 seconds ago are now descending, so he needs to get rid of the two clubs I just sent to him by also throwing them as double spins about three feet over his head.

If the top club in the multiplex triangle I threw lands in Steve's right hand with maddening precision and timing, and there have been no collisions, all five clubs will now be

---

[14] Two full rotations of the clubs while they're in the air.

Throwing Up – I Gatto Learn How to Juggle

in a cascade[15] pattern above Steve. I stand and watch, holding the unneeded sixth club, until Steve decides to drop out of the cascade by throwing every right hand catch back at me until we're back in a standard six-club passing pattern.

People get lured into this gravity-defying cult in a number of different ways, which have, mercifully, evolved over time.

During my first 20 years of juggling, judging by my casual observations,[16] the far and away most common path of entry into this hobby was out on a college campus lawn, between computer science classes.

Until fairly recently, juggling demographics broke down to roughly:
- 86 percent scientists, mathematicians, programmers, coders and your generalist nerds
- Six percent renaissance festival outcasts
- Five percent philosophy and theater majors
- Three percent everyone else[17]

Additionally, the juggling gender breakdown in the 80s and 90s was roughly:
- 99.4 percent men
- 0.6 percent everyone else

If you're thinking I'm exaggerating or trying to be funny here, as evidence of these claims, please go to YouTube and

---

[15] A "cascade" is a standard juggling pattern all jugglers use and is usually the pattern taught to novices.
[16] Which are akin to air-tight truth in this era, fact checker, so don't bother.
[17] This is where I land, obviously.

search for "Solving three cubes while juggling them." You don't have to watch all six minutes, but skip around and get the gist.

Are you back? Good. Let's cross-reference this scene with the North American Juggling Geek Master Checklist.
- ✓ College campus lawn
- ✓ Bunch of poorly dressed, young guys
- ✓ Guy is a juggler *and* a Rubik's Cube expert, meaning he's likely one of the Top 10 Geeks in the State of California, possibly the entire West Coast
- ✓ Juggler is a student at Stanford (T-shirt clue)
- ✓ Juggler is a Math major (learned via Google, because I just had to know)
- ✓ Shameless geek reinforcement by wearing a GoPro on head
- ✓ A socially awkward geek, oblivious to the juggler's need for total concentration to perform such a stunt, tries to engage juggler in pointless conversation

Never mind the stunt, which is undeniably impressive. What's truly remarkable about this scene is that there appear to be up to *three* women in the immediate area, which proves my point that juggling demographics are changing rapidly. In a similar scene set in 1988, the nearest woman would be, at minimum, 50 yards away, up-wind, facing the other direction.

You'd be forgiven for thinking to yourself "That damning evidence Leif just presented makes jugglers sound like a cabaret of socially awkward, insufferable weirdos." This was once painfully true. But, in the past 15 years or so, juggler demographics have changed dramatically! The juggling-as-a-sport momentum has attracted a strong field of legitimate badasses, from all genders. People are learning to juggle at younger ages, which, in addition to introducing a wider variety of backgrounds and interests outside of the geekpocalypse, has had the pleasing effect of producing more juggling gods than you can keep track of at clubs and festivals.

Learning to juggle as a kid has a multitude of advantages:
- You're a stupid kid with few inhibitions and almost no self-doubt, so you learn things infuriatingly fast.[18]
- You don't have a job or expenses to keep you from practicing for hours and hours everyday.
- You (probably) aren't distracted by hormonal urges yet.
- You don't get tired as quickly.

This makes for the perfect environment for kids to become much better jugglers at an earlier age. When you factor in that #KidsTheseDays[19] can obsessively study and build on the thousands and thousands of juggling videos readily available online, progress can be dazzlingly fast.

---

[18] From the perspective of a nearby adult, three weeks into practicing the same trick and not making much progress.
[19] Referenced so frequently in this book, it merits a hashtag.

In the 80s and 90s, there were only a handful of jugglers who, if they walked into the main gym at a juggling festival and started practicing, caused all activity around them to cease while people openly gawked in awe. These days, this caliber of juggler is pleasingly, almost unbelievably common. Do a slow, 360-degree rotation in the middle of a juggling festival now and there will be more people doing amazing things, landing tricks previously believed to be impossible and straight-up "holy shit what did I just see?" moments than you can keep track of.

As mentioned above, I entered the juggling community on an atypical track for the time. It went a little something like this:

From 1980-84, there was a TV show called "That's Incredible!" Each week, the hosts, Fran Tarkenton[20], John Davidson[21] and Cathy Lee Crosby[22] would do a couple stories about amazing/fascinating people, crazy stunts and other cool stuff. They would also do about a million stupid stories about boring things to fill out the hour—at least in the eyes of 12-year-old me.

The amazing stuff included:
- A guy that could karate chop a shot arrow in mid-air
- The tallest man and woman in the world

---

[20] Former Minnesota Vikings quarterback.
[21] Actor, singer and game show host.
[22] Actress and former pro tennis player.

- The shortest man and woman in the world
- A guy in China with two heads
- A guy that could chug an entire pitcher of beer while standing on his head in like two seconds
- Some lunatic that let a friend shoot a gun into his mouth while wearing a custom-made, bullet-proof throat guard that barely kept him from dying
- Freaky paranormal events that only stupid kids would believe
- A guy that could sit inside a tiny box for a really long time

The stupid stuff included:
- A new innovation in heart surgery that slightly increased the patient's quality of life
- Ditto eye surgery
- Some obscure astronomy discovery
- New technology that had nothing to do with robots
- Basically anything science or medical-related, that didn't involve a second head

"That's Incredible!" was the first TV show[23] that had to preview their stunt segments with a "don't try this at home" warning to keep idiots from accidentally killing themselves. It was awesome.

---

[23] Or one of the first.

In 1981, an 8-year-old kid named Antony Gatto[24] was on the show and blew my mind, juggling four and five balls, four and five rings, and three clubs that must have been at least half as long as he was. I'm not sure if I unthinkably, inexplicably missed the episode when it first aired or I caught a second appearance of the episode the following year, but it wasn't until summer of 1982, just after I turned 12, that I watched the show and said to myself "Screw it, I'm going to teach myself to juggle."[25]

So, I found three tennis balls, went out in my backyard and tried to figure out how to juggle. But there was one small problem; I had no idea what a juggling pattern looked like.

Cartoon juggling is always depicted as the balls flying around in a circle. I already knew that wasn't right, but beyond that I was clueless.

A standard juggling pattern that all (normal) people learn first is called a "cascade." A cascade pattern done correctly looks and behaves a lot like a figure-8 car racing track. A ball, in this case starting in the right hand, is thrown about two feet in the air over to the left hand diagonally across the middle of the pattern. Somewhere above the left hand, the ball reaches the peak of its arc and falls to the left

---

[24] Gatto went on to have a glorious career as a juggler, smashing records, winning awards and performing in such high-profile venues as *The Tonight Show*, Cirque du Soleil and many years in Las Vegas. He retired in 2013 at the age of 40 and opened a concrete business. He's widely considered to be one of the greatest jugglers in the history of the human race.
[25] Paraphrased.

hand. Then the left hand does a scooping motion from outside the sideways figure 8 to the inside as it launches the ball back into the air once again, about two feet high, diagonally across the middle where it peaks and falls back into the right hand. Add two more balls and that's juggling.

It looks like this.

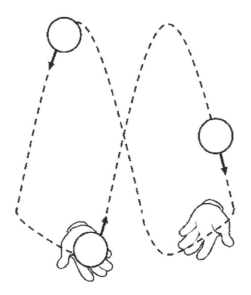

Despite the space in the middle being shared by balls constantly crisscrossing through it, the pattern works as long as the throws are accurate, timed correctly and you keep moving. If any of those three elements gets out of whack or interrupted, you risk collisions and the pattern falling apart —or at least becoming very difficult to maintain.

Described like this, or better yet demonstrated in person by a coach, juggling just becomes a matter of practice and, in the coaching situation, identifying problems and correcting them before they become ingrained as bad habits. I didn't have any of this assistance. I just knew balls needed to fly into the air in rhythm and not hit the ground. The rest was trial and error.

It should come as no surprise to hear that a 12-year-old with tennis balls,[26] no diagram to follow and no help, struggled to find a workable pattern. Hours upon hours were spent haphazardly throwing balls into the air and hoping they would somehow find the right trajectories themselves. When you do something like this for long enough, you eventually come tantalizingly close to something that's similar to juggling. While you still haven't figured out the correct pattern, your catching improves to the point where, with some luck, randomly thrown balls can be caught a few times. Though without order, this tactic rarely gets beyond four or five throws and catches before dropping ensues.

I probably could have developed a strong foundation in a second language in the time I spent out in the yard, throwing balls into the air, then clawing haplessly trying to catch more than one or two. Frequent collisions, and the bouncy nature of tennis balls, meant significant amounts of time chasing balls that ricocheted several feet away in opposite directions. Or into the bushes. Or over the fence.

My mission to juggle three balls may have also been hindered by the matter of my nearly complete lack of athleticism and more than a touch of clumsiness. Though I

---

[26] Tennis balls are actually terrible for learning to juggle. They're too light and bouncy. Find some beanbags.

was able to dribble a full-sized basketball while turning and talking as young as age 3, other kids quickly caught up and passed me in the realm of hand-eye coordination, sports and generally eluding situations that made one look like a klutzy buffoon.

Not only was I not gifted in any playground or organized sports, but it seemed I had a superpower for attracting any misfortune the universe was unleashing in my vicinity.

Take this example: One time in grade school, maybe fifth or sixth grade, as we were returning to class from a game of kickball, a kid kicked the ball super high in the air. I was about 30 feet away, along with a few other kids, not paying attention. In the space of that entire field, with numerous kids standing around, where did that ball land? Why squarely on my head, of course, with an accompanying, comically perfect "pwang" noise. The entire class erupted into fall-down, helpless laughter, as one would expect after something so ridiculously unlikely and cartoonish. Episodes like this filled my pre-teen years.

I was never going to be great at hockey, baseball, basketball, football or any other somethingball. While I'm luxuriating in the benefits today, looking especially young for my age wasn't doing me any favors in grade school and junior high. I was manifestly under-sized and weak for my age and I had the lung capacity of a fish on a hot sidewalk.

Organized sports at Brackett Field, my local park, was where I cemented my years-long, last-picked status for team games. I was so small that I was bumped down to the younger age group for hockey. I had a lock on the least likely to touch the ball positions on the soccer team. I was placed so deep in right field for baseball that kids, even some adults, couldn't have possibly hit the ball all the way to me. There was no after-school football at Brackett, thank Buddha, though even back then I was cognizant enough to form a strong argument as to how and why football was stupid.

It eventually became clear that if I was going to excel at anything, it was probably going to have to be something unorthodox. Something obscure enough that other kids weren't capable of judging whether I was gifted or sucked at it. Something that the neighborhood jocks couldn't walk up and, after five minutes, be able to do the thing better than I could. Something I could practice privately to work out all the inevitable freak, hilarious accidents and blows to the head before displaying the activity publicly. Juggling seemed perfect.

After about two weeks of dumb kid-caliber trial and error, marked by occasional violent spiking of balls into the ground in frustration and drop kicking them into the yard two houses away, I accidentally worked out the proper juggling pattern.[27]

With that ordeal behind me, I was hooked. Since a few weeks of interest in a new hobby wasn't quite enough to

---

[27] Researchers collecting evidence proving the Infinite Monkey Theorem are welcome to contact me.

inspire my parents to buy me real juggling props, I limped along with the ill-suited tennis balls for months. Progress was swift, thanks to the copious free time of a kid on summer vacation who didn't yet own an Atari 2600.

In just a few months of practicing in my yard, as I created a six-foot diameter circular bald spot in the grass, I tackled what I later learned were the standard, intuitive beginner tricks. These included throwing a single ball over the top of the pattern (rather than through it), throwing a single ball under the leg and, the novice juggler holy grail, behind the back. I'd also learned a few bounce tricks, because that's what tennis balls do best, like a single bounce, two and three bounces in a row and a simultaneous two ball bounce. Soon I'd progressed from three to four balls, which isn't a huge leap in skill, but it sure got 12-year-old me pumped.

Out of desperation to try news things, I even tried to fashion juggling rings out of cardboard. Unsurprisingly, they only survived a few drops before they were so contorted as to be un-jugglable. I desperately needed proper gear to take my juggling to the next level and I already knew convincing my parents to buy that gear was not going to be easy.

My parents had already made themselves, and by extension me, famous throughout all of South Minneapolis with their passion for repurposing old sporting equipment instead of buying new stuff. This was most notoriously exemplified by my first bicycle and baseball glove, both of them hand-me-downs from my father, circa the early-1950s.

The bike was a legitimate WWII-era antique that, if they had waited another decade and cleaned it up a bit, probably could have been sold to a collector for a respectable price. Meanwhile, the oversized, over-padded baseball glove was almost as big as my torso. Out on the field, I looked like one of the kids from the Peanuts cartoon.

That's me on the left, on the world's most low self-esteem bike.

I plugged away, determined to take my juggling to the next level. Being that I had zero reference to work with, all new tricks and innovation were of the reinvent-the-wheel variety.

Some friend of the family eventually took pity on me and bought me a copy of the wildly popular book "Juggling for the Complete Klutz,"[28] including the attached mesh sack of honest-to-goodness beanbags. The beanbags made my life easier, but I struggled with the written directions and diagrams in the book. I needed something more visual. I pressed on with my trial-and-error method.

 Fortunately, salvation was at hand. In the winter of 1982, I tagged along with my dad to a meeting of his cycling club at nearby Matthews Park. My mom encouraged me to ask at the front desk if the park knew about any juggling classes or clubs. As it turned out, there was a juggling club that met at Matthews every Monday. It happened to be a Monday and the juggling club was meeting right then!

 I walked into the room where the jugglers were practicing and into a whole new world, like someone from the present getting zapped through a dimensional gate, straight onto the bridge of the starship Enterprise as Pickard is making first contact with a five-headed, talking squirrel. Suddenly, I had camaraderie and people to teach me new stuff. I was the only kid and I could sense that not everyone was thrilled about a kid invading their adult space, but I was too kid-like to care.

 My progress accelerated. I learned new tricks faster with people there to inspire me and show me how the patterns worked. As a result, my parents accidentally saddled themselves with the new chore of driving me to and picking me up from the park every Monday night for the next four years until I got my driver's license.

---

[28] First published in 1977, this book has sold over 2.5 million copies.

After roughly another six months and who knows how much nagging, I convinced my parents that I needed legit juggling props. Thanks to my new friends at the club, I knew there were exactly two places in Minneapolis to buy props: a novelty store out at a distant mall and a shop in downtown Minneapolis called Eagle Magic.

Eagle Magic, now long gone, but formerly located just two blocks from where I live today, had a tiny section reserved for juggling props among their rows of readymade magic tricks. Because of my relative newness to juggling, my parents weren't quite ready to invest in the Rolls Royce of juggling props. Also, I was still borderline too small to handle the really nice, larger juggling clubs anyway. And, though I had a history of treating my toys gently, there were probably still concerns that I would whip one of my new juggling clubs high into the air over concrete in an effort to entertain other kids and destroy it when I missed the catch. I ended up going home with a kind of Mattel version of juggling clubs, balls and rings, called JuggleBug.

JuggleBug may still be around today, though it's difficult to say. If they're still in business, they're somehow doing it without having fully embraced social media or even a useful website. Back in the early-80s, these were about the cheapest props you could buy that weren't straight-up toys. To be fair, the "good" juggling clubs of the era were really expensive and, because club design and construction was still evolving, they tended to break relatively easily.[29]

Clubs in the early 1980s were thick, super hard plastic on the outside and hollow on the inside reinforced by a wooden dowel, which hurt like hell when they landed funny. All it took was your hand being a fraction of an inch off target for smashed and bloody thumbs and finger tips.

I soon learned this club design was considerably less painful and potentially concussive than the one-piece, solid, super heavy clubs people were using before the 1970s. Occasionally someone at juggling club would pull out an old set of these monsters. Even just holding one of them gave me pause. One time I managed to work up the nerve to juggle them. They were so heavy, and my arms were so twig-like, that it was difficult to even get a juggling pattern started. Ten seconds of those things spinning close to my face made me grateful for the mere bruised hands and bleeding fingers tips I was suffering as opposed to fractured skulls and snapped radial bones. I don't have stats on the mortality rate for jugglers in the early 20th-century, but I'm willing to bet most jugglers didn't make it to retirement without at least three broken noses.

Another factor that led to the initial purchase of JuggleBug clubs was the expensive kind were longer than JuggleBugs, so when a tiny person like me juggled them,

---

[29] The multi-piece club with a cushioned handle and foam caps on the ends, which nearly all jugglers use today, first appeared in about 1969. This style of club was still very much in its design adolescence when I started shopping for clubs in 1983.

there were a lot of wood-on-bone thwacks to my forearms and collarbones when things went awry. And despite the great leaps in club design, they were still heavy enough that a direct blow to the head was reasonably dangerous for someone whose skull had only recently finished hardening.

A year and change after learning to juggle, my first, and perhaps greatest, juggling claim to fame occurred. Probably hoping to suck in some of that sweet "Juggling for the Complete Klutz" payday, a local game company called Jax, which still exists, decided to design and sell a poor man's answer to Klutz with their own pancake-like beanbags, with rudimentary juggling instructions on the package in lieu of a book. The product was called, I shit you not, "Original Jugalo." The balls inside were called "Jugalobes."

In order to illustrate how easy it was to learn how to juggle, thus inspiring kids to torment their parents for the impulse buy in the checkout line, they needed a picture of a kid on the package, juggling and looking like he was having the goddamn time of his life. I'd like to say I beat out 1,000 other kids at a grueling casting cattle call, but as it turned out I was the only kid juggler in Minnesota at the time. Between putting me or an illustration on the cover, they chose me. Even better, though I was 13-years-old at the time, I still looked about 9 or 10.[30] I was born for this gig. I was the Original Jugalo.[31]

For the picture, the company actually wanted me to do the circular juggling pattern I described earlier that you see in cartoons. Like tunnel-vision marketing people everywhere, they were immune to the plain evidence that this was not how a standard juggling pattern worked. The circular pattern is actually a trick called a "shower"[32] and, as luck would have it, I had learned to do it just a few weeks earlier.

This was also my first experience trying to juggle under bright lights. Lighting is a ceaseless liability for jugglers, particularly when performing on stage, because no matter which way you turn, you're probably being blasted right in the eye holes by flood and/or spotlights. Naturally, this makes it difficult to see, and a key component of juggling is keeping tabs on where several objects are flying at all times. Jugglers performing outside have different challenges, mainly if the sun is facing the stage, but also on those lightly overcast days where the sunlight is so powerfully diffused that it makes your eyes water to look *anywhere* in the sky.

_____

[30] I suffered with being the smallest kid in my class all the way up until I turned 16, when I exploded into the nearly average-sized human I am today.

[31] As far as I'm concerned, the Insane Clown Posse owes me like a million dollars. And yes, I plan to have "Original Jugalo" carved onto my gravestone.

[32] Don't ask me why. It's also sometimes called a "fountain," which makes more sense.

Throwing Up – I Gatto Learn How to Juggle

A black-and-white test shot before shooting in color.

Photo studios are even worse. The subject is surrounded by giant flash lighting kits (which were gianter and flashier in the early 1980s). I stood in the center of the room, juggling those wobbly, pancake beanbags with expensive equipment surrounding me on all sides, trying to run a trick I had just learned. Every time the photographer snapped a picture, the whole studio went supernova for an instant, leaving me seeing spots and causing me to drop. I had to shake off temporary blindness after each photo. Fortunately, those floppy beanbags plopped firmly on the ground when I dropped them without bouncing or rolling, so there was no time wasted chasing them around the studio. If the photo shoot had been with tennis balls, we would have been there all night.

Even so, I imagine my inability to juggle blind made the photographer late for dinner, but we came away with the perfect photo. Several weeks later, someone brought one of the first packages of Jugalos with my cute face on the top-right side of the package to juggling club and I basked in the ensuing fame.

My payment for the photo shoot was $100, plus a box of Jugalos. I gave the Jugalos as treasured gifts to people for years. I keep one beat up package on my bookshelf.

I was the early and mid-80s version of the #KidsTheseDays that I faux-loathe now. I learned new tricks quickly, openly annoying the adult jugglers around me who, for all I knew, talked smack about me while drinking beer instead of practicing. Little did I know that in about 15 years, those situations would be reversed. It's the circle of juggling life.

Coming of Age

"Close Game" – Duration: 5.7 seconds
I've forgotten why we named this trick "Close Game." Perhaps because the entire thing requires some truly heroic catching by both of us, meaning it's constantly close to failure.

Steve gathers two clubs in his right hand during standard six-club passing and tosses them at me sideways, over his head, like a basketball hook shot. If the clubs are still reasonably close together when they get to me, I scoop catch both of them in one move with my left hand. The next few tenths of seconds are particularly action-packed. I quickly transfer these two clubs to my right hand, while making small, sometimes not small, adjustments to their position so they're in just the right placement, which will become important in about half a second. I catch the next incoming throw from Steve in my left hand and place that on top of the two clubs already in my right hand. Now they're ready for a three-club multiplex throw back to Steve.

If we hadn't lost our collective minds so many years ago, I'd throw a "normal" three-club multiplex[33] back at Steve. But, as we often conclude while designing new tricks, that would be too easy. Instead, I twist and contort my body to make space for me to throw that three-club multiplex

---

[33] I should point out that very, very few people in the world throw three-club multiplexes while club passing, in any configuration. While not unique, this is one of our signature tricks.

behind my back to Steve. This usually isn't pretty, so Steve has to look especially alive at this moment and catch all three clubs, in any number of hectic ways, sometimes while seeing his life flash before his eyes.

Being a juggling prodigy in junior high wasn't winning me any popularity contests. I was still among the smallest kids in the whole school, I still had a funny name, ripe for multifaceted mocking, and I still sucked at just about all the activities that makes one cool in junior high.

    I was too small, weak and slow for most sports. I was too clueless to hang with the rapidly emerging computer geek clique. I wasn't good looking enough to be the hot guy, I wasn't smart enough to be a nerd and I wasn't funny enough to be the comedian. I was, however, as previously illustrated, unintentionally funny enough on some occasions to be the clown, so I had that going for me.

    My growing juggling skills were putting me in a kind of helpless Peter Parker predicament as I had no opportunity to impress my peers with my new superpowers. Everyone else had a platform to demonstrate their respective strengths: class, band, after-school sports and so on. There was no place during or after school for a large group of my peers to watch me do some slick juggling tricks, definitively demonstrating that I was the best juggler they knew and cashing in on what I imagined to be top-shelf notoriety. Even bringing it up in casual conversation was hopeless. Guess how many social points you earn if you walk up to a group of junior high school kids talking about their various scholastic achievements or sporting victories, lean in and say "By the way, I'm a pretty good juggler." Negative a million, that's how many.

While juggling wasn't making me popular, it was beginning to have small effects on my life. One day, slumped in my chair during an idle moment in eighth grade Earth science class, I happened to look down at my dangling arm. I noticed for the first time that my forearm, once perfectly thin and straight like a pipe, had developed a small bulge just below the elbow. A muscle! A small, well-defined muscle! And veins! There were bulging veins running up and down my forearm! When did they get there? My days of being the weakest kid in a 10-mile radius were slowly coming to a close.

High school was a different story. Within two months of starting my freshman year, I went from being an anonymous pipsqueak, still clinging to a grade school bowl haircut, to being "that kid that juggles." I was launched to this plane of dubious popularity via the 1984 homecoming talent show.

The homecoming talent show wasn't just for theater geeks, because this event was also when they crowned the homecoming king and queen. That meant the popular kids had to show up, too. And the aspiring popular kids. And the sportos, scholastic overachievers, and pretty much everyone else outside of the Goths, dweebs and wasteoids. It was the perfect vehicle to show off my secret mad skillz and not look like an attention-starved loser while doing it.

By this stage, I'd been juggling long enough to have a pretty solid five minutes of tricks I could do to background music. I needed a song that was suitably long and high energy. Since this was 1984 in Minnesota, the choice was clear, Prince's "1999."

The audience was something like 17 times larger than any audience I'd been in front of before. And it only dawned on me right before the show that I would be spending one to four years with these people. That's a long time to be around kids that saw me faint from stage fright, fire-hose barf all over the homecoming royalty or some other Leif-caliber catastro-suck.

Thankfully, not only did I not evacuate my bladder (though it was close), but I also didn't humiliate myself. I juggled three, four and five balls, three and four clubs, juggled a bowling ball, baseball bat and hacky sack, and did a short routine with spinning balls.

However, in a cruel twist, I wasn't the only juggler in the talent show. A senior also performed—a flamboyant theater/choir geek, naturally—whom I'd met before through the juggling club. He totally upstaged me by juggling torches.

Along with machetes, torches are one of the greatest rube-pleasing tricks in juggling. There's no danger, people. Let me amend that. If you happened to throw an errant torch that ignited your hairspray (this was the 80s, after all), which caused you to panic and trip over your gas can, which you carelessly left uncapped, which spilled and was then ignited by your hair fireball, and you rolled around in the flame pool for a few seconds for some reason, *that* would be dangerous. Otherwise, your biggest worry when juggling torches is minimizing the amount of soot you get on your clothes.

 Despite being shown up by that shameless audience-pandering drivel, the whole school gave me high fives the next morning and I scored a coveted picture in the yearbook.[34] I would end up performing in all four of the homecoming talent shows while I was in high school and a few of the spring talent shows as well.

Sophomore year I mercifully shot up past the 5-foot barrier and well into triple digits in weight—much of it muscle. I could bench press 30 pounds over my body weight, which is really saying something when you weigh less than 120 pounds. In addition to the noticeable impact juggling was having on my body, there were also not so noticeable transformations, namely my reflexes, hand speed and dexterity. I wasn't beefy enough to take up basketball or football, but things like wrestling and track and field seemed right up my alley.

 The pole vaulting coach tracked me down and recruited me my sophomore year, based on feats of strength and body control he'd seen during wrestling practice. I

---
[34] Immortalizing that soon-discarded bowl cut well into 1985.

wasn't a particularly fast runner (I was all upper body), an important element of pole vaulting, but I was able to compensate by muscling my way over the cross bar. Alas, in the long term, this bad form caused all manner of back pain that persisted well into my 20s.[35]

While all this physical development was happening around age 15, for reasons that defy explanation to this day, virtually everyone simultaneously decided my name was cool instead of hilarious. The least miserable school years of my life, up to that point, had begun just in time for all-important high school socializing.

This isn't to say that I was in the top 50 popular kids in high school – or the top 100. Since my popularity was late to bloom, I wasn't deeply embedded in any existing cliques, so there was no Leif groundswell of support for things like team captains and homecoming royalty. Instead, I was accepted as kind of a floater into almost all social groups. You know, like a small thing that can fly from social group to social group, landing, enjoying that group's nectar like a butterfly, and taking off again. If only there was a convenient term for that phenomenon.

Wanting to develop my juggling prowess further, I needed to find a space where I could practice for more than just two hours every Monday night at Matthews Park. Since the school gyms were all spoken for by after school sports, I took ownership of the wide open spaces and high ceilings in the lunch room. This endeared me not only to other people

---

[35] Good form is better than strength, folks, every time.

loitering after school, but also the staff who didn't flee the school at the stroke of the final bell. Even the much reviled vice principal accosted me one day for a short lesson.[36]

High school was also when I got my first significant taste of paid performing. Gigs usually consisted of birthday parties and neighborhood carnivals, though I was occasionally called to help out the University of Minnesota Juggling Club for basketball halftime shows and other large group performing events. There were many professional jugglers in the Twin Cities, which I'd convinced myself was the best job ever, and I began paying attention to their methods for my promising future in performing.

---

[36] She was just OK.

Doing a show at a retirement home (circa 1987)

    I drifted toward the pro jugglers at the club, including "Jons The Juggler" and the late comedian/juggler Scott Burton. Jons in particular was a key influence. Jons worked with troubled inner-city youth, so his instincts were to encourage all the dumb kids around him instead of politely avoiding them, like most adult jugglers during my early and middle teen years. He let me tag along to many of his shows and even took me to the Minnesota Renaissance Festival a couple times, where he performed for years, so I could see even more juggling acts.

Another key juggling influence and inspiration in the mid/late 1980s were The Flying Karamazov Brothers. The Karamazovs, a five-man juggling troupe who to my knowledge never flew and were not brothers, would blow into Minneapolis about once a year and perform sold-out shows at the legendary Guthrie Theater. This was the first high production value, fancy venue-worthy, two-hour juggling act I'd ever seen. They had sets and costumes and musical instruments and weird props that did not look easy or cheap to make.

The Karamazovs had two signature bits. One was called "The Gamble," where one brother would juggle any three items tossed up onto the stage by the audience after a dramatic build-up. Naturally, after the first few years when keys, wallets, hats, shoes, umbrellas and other everyday items were offered, audiences started coming prepared. I have memories of people bringing up golf clubs, an armed rat trap, heavy chains dripping with grease and an inflated balloon partly filled with beans.[37] One year three guys heaved an ottoman-sized boulder onto the stage, which was immediately disqualified.[38]

The rapidly increasing absurdity of items smirking people brought on stage for The Gamble compelled the Brothers to set ground rules. The submission criteria for objects were:

---
[37] Amazingly, the only time I ever saw the Brothers fail The Gamble challenge was because of this exquisitely simple, but evil object.
[38] Can you believe the Guthrie let people bring a *boulder* into their theater without some kind of security incident? God, I miss the 80s.

1. Must weigh more than an ounce (28 grams)
2. Must weigh less than 10 pounds (4.5 kg)
3. Must be no bigger than a breadbox
4. Must not be a live animal
5. Must not be able to stop the "Champ" from being a live animal[39]

The Brothers' other signature bit was an interlude of unscripted club passing they called "Jazz." Or maybe it was "Jazz Passing." Who cares. The important thing is this bit, which I suspect may have been conceived of so the Brothers could insert a wee bit of variety into the otherwise monotonous task of performing the same show 189 times a year, was simply the group passing clubs and throwing random tricks at each other. This would often get lively as tricks got more and more wild, timing and rhythm decayed and, I suspect, the Brothers made unsubtle attempts to make each other drop.

Does this style of lawless, spontaneous club passing sound vaguely familiar? I don't recall it being a conscious choice 25-something years ago when Steve and I first started juggling together, but it wouldn't be a stretch to suggest that the batshit crazy Duck and Cover style of club passing can be traced back to this bit.

The only other way to see examples of juggling from outside the Twin Cities bubble in the 1980s were the precious few VHS juggling tapes circulating among club members. I studied these performances closely, sometimes

---
[39] Source: Wikipedia.

advancing the tape frame-by-frame in an attempt to absorb all the subtle movements in every trick. Then I would go to the gym, take those tricks and put a new spin on them to make them my own.

For example, lots of jugglers were juggling three clubs up over their heads. Not only did I want to be different, but honestly having three clubs spinning just above my face was terrifying. Instead I juggled three clubs above my head using flat throws—when clubs remain horizontal throughout their flight. Doing flat throws down in the normal juggling configuration was a popular trick. By combining the two tricks, and reducing the possibility of a broken nose in the process, I'd created a trick no one else did. Decades later, I'm not sure I've ever seen anyone but me do that trick. This was just the first flicker of me using this technique to invent new tricks, which I would, and still, lean on for developing new club passing tricks with Steve.

It was about this time that I got the idea in my head that I could be a really great juggler. I would read about competitors' routines in the juniors[40] competitions at the International Jugglers' Association (IJA) annual festival and championships and think to myself, "I'm better than that kid. I'm better than that kid, too!" Alas, I wouldn't get the opportunity to attend an IJA festival until I was 19 years old, thus a senior competitor, and wildly out-classed by the field of pro jugglers.

---

[40] Ages 17 and under.

Fortunately, I had certifiable jock Scott Burton to emulate in the meantime. Scott was the most skilled juggler in my realm of awareness before I attended an IJA festival. This meant he was at the center of my juggling ambitions for years. Scott had a unique juggling style for the time, and still rare today, where each trick was followed immediately by another trick. There were no pauses to gather himself or correct a bad throw. Not even a single self-throw. Just trick, trick, trick, trick. If he dropped in practice, he'd start the *entire* routine from the beginning again instead of picking up where he left off like us mortals.

Scott practiced so relentlessly that he came to juggling club one night with a glove on his right hand. He said needed the glove, because his palm between his thumb and forefinger was so beat-up from absorbing tens of thousands of blows from catching clubs every day that it had begun to decay and grow some kind of fungus. To this day, that is the most badass juggling injury I have ever seen.

I wanted so much to be like Scott. I wanted to be a full-time performer and book both standard juggling shows and comedy clubs. I wanted to have a breathtaking four-club routine and juggle five clubs.[41] I wanted to have a disgusting, alarming thing on my hand from practicing too hard and then *keep practicing* anyway.

But I was still a kid with kid limitations and frivolous kid commitments, like graduating high school. Even in a best case scenario, I was several years away from even

---
[41] He was the one and only person I saw juggle five clubs for years.

starting my career as a Scott Burton. So, I nobly soldiered on, finished high school and started classes at the University of Minnesota, where I entered into the "professional show off" phase—and a much larger world of juggling.

My high school senior photo (1988). If you look closely, you can see that I'm kneeling, because the ceiling in the photo studio was too low for me to juggle four clubs while standing. Also, check out my little tribute to Scott Burton with the gloves.

Professional Show Off

"Bat to the Bounce" – Duration: 2.2 seconds
This is perhaps one of the top three most dangerous tricks that Steve and I have ever done.

It's fairly simple, if you disregard that Steve should be wearing full hockey goalie pads. Steve tosses a one-and-a-half spin club from his right hand, over the top of the passing pattern to my right hand. With the club I'm holding in my right hand, I "bat" (it's more like a "smash") the incoming club down to the floor, back toward Steve. If nothing has gone wrong with Steve's precision throw or my wild bat, the club will hit the floor, then leap back up, totally out of control and traveling at roughly the speed of light. If severe injury doesn't seem imminent, or worse, incipient, Steve will attempt to catch the club in whatever hand is most convenient.

If anything has gone wrong, well, I'm just glad Steve is on the receiving end.[42]

Until juggling becomes a lucrative sport, at its essence it's simply a great excuse to show off. If anyone out there disagrees with me, answer me this question: Have you ever juggled in front of other people? Then you were showing off.

After suffering through awesomeness anonymity in junior high school, then coming out as a juggler in high

---

[42] For the record, my memory is that this trick was entirely Steve's idea, so my conscience is clear.

school, I was ready to really commit during my university years.

The University of Minnesota Juggling Club opened up all manner of opportunities. For starters, they had two formal meetings each week in the enormous Peik Gym on the edge of the East Bank campus, allowing for more practice time in poor weather.

In good weather, however, spontaneous juggling club meetings were frequent, even if it was just me, out on the university's grassy Mall, surrounded by buildings whose protection made wind less of a headache. Also, when I juggled on the Mall, girls could see. The only nuisance were the alarmingly bold squirrels who, in addition to sandwiches people were holding *in their hands*, were prone to prancing up, stealing a bean bag and taking it 20 feet up into a tree to nibble it to death.

If you'll remember from earlier, the number of women in juggling circles in the 1980s was... sparse. And, in most cases, the women who were present were either someone's wife or under-aged daughter. The U of M Mall was crawling with age-appropriate women, walking by, lying in the sun, studying in the shade and, we hoped, side-eye watching us display a form of juggling (i.e. not clowning) that they had likely never seen before.

Still, even in athletic, technically difficult form, juggling wasn't making most women swoon with admiration. But a small percentage would stop and watch and even that scant attention was better than what was normally available in the juggleverse, opposite sex-wise, so we were happy.

The U of M Juggling Club also had a giant stockpile of equipment to play with, meaning one could dabble and experiment with new props without having to cough up the money to buy them. For example, I was able to try, and then never try again, riding what turned out to be a frightening six-foot unicycle.

Finally, the club was also admirably organized in terms of outreach and opportunities. We were frequently called upon to perform, usually for money, at events on campus and around town. Not only did this allow club members to collect more on-stage experience without having to go solo and hustle for shows, but that money was reinvested in the club to buy new equipment, fund parties and even help send people to the International Jugglers' Association annual festival. This financial assistance is how I found myself at my first ever IJA festival in Baltimore in 1989.

The university juggling club's IJA fund wasn't enough to buy me an airplane ticket to the 1989 festival, which is how I ended up in a 22-hour car ride with Jeff.

Jeff was a local who had shot to juggling stardom in a relatively short amount of time. I had never seen anyone progress as fast as Jeff had. With copious natural ability and a fierce practice regime, he'd gone from novice to juggling superstar in only four or five years.

Unfortunately, this talent was paired with a breathtaking level of arrogance the likes of which I had never seen in my 19 years. Jeff was capable of being amenable for long periods, even generous, but these instances were broken up by moments of undisguised self-importance and dickishness that never failed to stun me. Being that he was so quick and unapologetic about whipping out this behavior, one has to assume this attitude was cultivated and tolerated much farther back than his ascension to juggling greatness.

Unsurprisingly, paired with this ego was his loathing of anyone who might threaten said ego. Anthony Gatto, then only 16-years-old, attended the 1989 festival in Baltimore as well. Even at that age, he was regarded as one of the greatest jugglers who had ever lived. Whenever Anthony entered the gym to practice, everyone stopped what they were doing, encircled him, sat down and gawked. Everyone except Jeff, that is, who was openly repulsed by this lavish fawning over someone who wasn't him. Jeff kept on juggling, all alone, on the other side of the gym while we watched Gatto.

I was no Jeff, but I was still considered to be one of the hot young phenoms. I was one of the very few people who could juggle five clubs and (barely) juggle seven balls at the time. That didn't diminish the awe I experienced at the festival. I had never been in a room with so many jugglers before—hundreds and hundreds of them, ranging from beginners to pros. I attended workshops on juggling large numbers of objects, performing, comedy, new props and more. I watched Cindy Marvell become the first woman to ever win the IJA championships.

I was also introduced to the edgier, adults-only side of juggling in Baltimore. The "Renegade" show is held in the evenings at all IJA festivals, starting between 11 p.m. and midnight, either at a bar or someplace where the sale of alcohol is permitted and bartenders don't cut you off, no matter how shitfaced you get. Needless to say, drunken chaos paired with people capable of performing amazing feats can lead to a lot of spontaneous bad decisions.

The Renegade stage was (and sometimes still is) where people did dangerous things, vulgar things, took off their clothes, set stuff on fire that wasn't meant to be set on fire then throw the flaming item into the audience and other activities that sensible people don't do.

Renegade has evolved over the years. The potential danger to spectators has been put in check. Also, the possibility of suffering drunken heckling and public humiliation has diminished considerably. In the 80s and 90s, if you sucked, or you were taking too long, or if you were taking too long to do something that sucked, the crowd would start to clap rhythmically. It started slow and built speed and volume until either the performer saved themselves by doing something unexpectedly wonderful or they were forced to leave the stage. It could be brutal and feelings were hurt, especially for people that hadn't been to Renegade before and thought they'd show off their work-in-progress, carnival clown show act.

These days Renegade can be hit or miss. The acts allowed on stage are vetted slightly better, which usually averts the potential for energy-draining tedium, but also this generation of jugglers is just nicer. Clapping people off stage happens rarely, if ever. The drunken shouting is usually encouragement, instead of heckling. Probably for the best, I suppose.

Perhaps I've just become a cynical old fart, but the electrifying spirit of Renegade is largely gone. There are still wonderful acts now and again, but the open encouragement of offensive, tasteless, semi-illegal hijinks isn't the same.

I should add in full disclosure that I've turned into one of those guys that enjoys eight hours of sleep more than seeing three, two-foot dildos being juggled by a burlesque dancer, reciting a dirty limerick, at 1:30 in the morning. So, perhaps I'm a poor judge.

I came home from Baltimore dazzled and energized. Not just from the insane amount of talent I'd witnessed—Minnesota had Scott Burton, Bryan Wendling, Tuey Wilson, frequent visits by the Passing Zone[43] and Jeff, after all—but by the exposure to new people and juggling sub-disciplines, the expanded juggling community and the pure joy everyone got from doing this activity together.

Back at the U of M Juggling Club, I rededicated myself to practicing as much as my classes and job would

---

[43] For the non-jugglers, these names probably won't mean much, but just trust me when I say they were some of the best jugglers in the world at the time.

allow. I was more convinced than ever that I would eventually go pro.

I have a storied history of getting wildly amped about an idea or project, only to find out it sucked. Professional juggling is right at the top of that list.[44]

At any level, professional juggling is a rough gig. Over time, I began to appreciate that it's a career path best suited for the masochistic, disturbingly optimistic and/or otherwise unemployable. Much like the music industry, when you reach the absolute pinnacle of your field, it's actually pretty lucrative.[45] But before that stage, it's a less homicidal "Mad Max: Fury Road" lifestyle, sharing vans with unwashed, farting, snoring guys, gas station burritos and money-saving squalor while displaying your hard-earned talent at Renaissance festivals, birthday parties for tiny humans and street performing for small bills and loose change. But I've gotten ahead of myself.

While I was still in college, I managed to land a local talent agent who started sending me out to do mostly small-time starter shows. The performing juggler food chain bottoms out with neighborhood carnivals (both walk-around juggling and performing for like eight people on whatever stage they've nailed together), birthday parties for little

---

[44] Spoiler alert.
[45] Namely the high side of corporate gigs, Vegas shows and crushingly boring, but well-paid cruise ships.

sadists, high school lock-ins and the occasional bottom-tier corporate show.

Considering what I was making at my part-time university job, the money I earned from the shows was pretty respectable.

Even with all the pros in Minneapolis to watch and learn about the many facets of full-time juggling, there were frustrating setbacks along the way. One in particular happened right out of the gate.

Back in the 1980s, the only way to efficiently spread your contact details to others was business cards. Getting them printed was a bit pricey, especially for a college freshman making $4.00 an hour at a chain pizza joint, but they were essential for self-promotion, so I bit the bullet.

I have never been a good speller and, unless I'm really focused, not a great proofreader either. In my junior year of college, I would learn that I had a touch of dyslexia, which, among other things, had me reversing letters and numbers, making it difficult for me to write words correctly and identify typos. My handwriting was so slow, illegible and full of bizarre typos,[46] my notes taken in lectures were nearly useless if I didn't go back and clean them up immediately after class while my memory was fresh.

If laptops and, more importantly, spell-checking software hadn't been invented, I'd probably be digging

---

[46] To this day, when handwriting, I still frequently swap neighboring letters in a word, particularly the first two letters. The same is true for typing. Or perhaps I'm just a really poor typist.

ditches somewhere instead of spending the last two decades being paid to write stuff.

This is a very long-winded way of explaining why, when I submitted the design and layout for my first juggling business cards, I spelled it "juging." The business card place had a strict policy of printing *exactly* what they received on the layout, no matter how obviously erroneous. They also apparently, despite the steep printing price, couldn't be bothered to do 30 seconds of legwork and pick up a phone to check with the customer whether they had meant to write "juging," instead of "juggling." How were they supposed to know "juging" isn't what I meant, the clerk said defensively when I picked up my cards? Like, maybe it was a joke? Or maybe there was this new performance art that looked like juggling,[47] but was instead called "juging."

As I said, I was destitute, and printing cards was not cheap, so I had to limp along with this embarrassing business card typo for nearly a year before they were replaced.

That same year, I learned that there were shows one should promptly decline. This lesson was learned when another juggler tricked me via withheld information into being his opening act for a giant conference of teenaged pro-life

---

[47] The card layout had a silhouette of me juggling five clubs, just in case there was any question about whether I was indeed doing something called "juging" for large audiences.

activists.[48] I was still a little naïve about the inflexibility and gravity of the pro-choice/life debate at that age, but I had somehow gleaned a kind of guarded intuition, kind of like puppies who selectively decide which strangers they like and which strangers make them cry.[49] I sensed there was something amiss going on underneath all those super-friendly, vacant-eyed, Jesus-praising facades and was very happy to get out of there.

On our way home, that juggler ran out of gas and I was left to sit freezing in the car in the dead of winter, parked on the side of a road with a high speed limit and almost no shoulder, while he hitchhiked to buy a can of gas. Fun times!

On the topic of close calls with pseudo-cults via juggling: Many months later I would attend a performance by a well-known juggler, whose name rhymes with "Fandy Lead." The show was at an area church a high school acquaintance attended, and she kindly thought to invite me. An earnest man I met that night spent the next six months aggressively trying to recruit me into what I came to realize was a full-on cult.[50] Those two encounters pretty much locked in my life-long atheism.

---

[48] In my defense, the gig paid really well and, again, I was barely getting by, so...
[49] This didn't stop me from accepting a "Pro Life" T-shirt from one of the perky ringleaders, which I'd hoped to doctor into saying "Pro Leif," but never got around to it.
[50] Thanks for that, Fandy.

The allure of easy money kept me going for a while, but eventually it dawned on me that performing was causing me to hate juggling. The problem with performing for civilians,[51] then and now, is that all they want to see is the juggler eat the apple.

For you non-jugglers, "eat-the-apple" is both a trick[52] and a shorthand term for all the lame juggling tricks that typical civilians think are the pinnacle of juggling skill. In addition to the aforementioned myth about the danger of juggling torches, some of the stupid tricks that civilians erroneously think are amazing include:

- Throwing an object really high and catching it
- Juggling really fast
- Cracking a whip (not while juggling)
- Juggling knives/machetes/axes or anything else purported to be "sharp" (they're not sharp)
- Juggling chainsaws (the chain has been removed, reducing it to a super-dull saw with a handle)
- Juggling odd objects (in my case a bowling ball, a baseball bat and a hacky sack, a trick I mastered in about 10 minutes)
- Juggling three bowling balls, because that's a surefire way to get a concussion, so anyone trying

---

[51] How some people refer to non-jugglers. Or maybe it's just me. Whatever, civilian.

[52] When someone juggles two balls and an apple and proceeds to eat the apple down to the core without interrupting the juggling pattern, usually making a giant slobbering mess in the process that little kids go batshit for.

it must be an idiot and thus deserves everything bad thing that happens to him or her (but probably not "her," because women are too smart to try something so stupid)

Juggling blindfolded, among the more difficult audience-pleasing tricks (circa 1991)

This cheap-thrill sullying of my distinguished art form aside, performing these tricks meant sacrificing a fair portion of my juggling free time to practice them, rather than working on fun tricks. I began to loathe doing shows, but again the money was easy, so I soldiered on until I suffered one too many birthday party humiliations.

Not all, but at most birthday parties, the kids did not give one bean-sized shit about watching a juggler. Part of the problem is that kids are little jerks and should all be marooned on a distant island until they turn 18 (girls) or 23 (boys), but some of the blame belongs to the parents.

By way of introduction, the well-meaning parent, sleep-deprived and probably suffering from a serious vitamin deficiency, would leap up and announce:

> "OK everyone! It's almost time to eat that giant chocolate cake you've all been drooling over for two hours, but first let's watch this poor college student juggle for 25 minutes!"

If memory serves, an ear-splitting, mass cry of anguish would follow. The kids would grumpily plop down on the grass in front of me, arms crossed, some of them sobbing quietly having realized for the first time that life is relentlessly unfair, then spend the entire show heckling me. Common remarks interrupting my patter included "Why aren't you wearing clown make-up?" "Can you juggle [one more object than the number of objects I was currently juggling]?" And the inevitable, "Throw it higher!!"

After less than two years, I walked away from performing, instead taking on a weekend job as a wedding DJ, effectively a lateral move in terms of shame money.

The desire for extra pocket money combined with a splash of masochism inspired me to try street performing while I was backpacking in Europe.

I had never tried solo street performing in the U.S. At the time, it was illegal in Minneapolis to perform in public places and ask for money afterward without a permit. Other cities, like San Francisco, had a highly regimented schedule based on seniority for performers on Pier 39, including stories of interlopers being aggressively bounced from the area by said performers.

Europe, as far as I could tell, was a free-for-all in the 1990s. Street performers were present, but they weren't nearly as territorial about performing spots or as pushy when passing the hat. And street performing hadn't yet grown into the spectacle it is today, where you practically have to bring out a live dinosaur to eat a smaller live dinosaur to get peoples' attention.[53]

My first attempt was on Oslo's Karl Johan Gate (Street), a quaint pedestrian lane through the heart of the city's retail district. Even though I only had a small bag of props, with no slack rope or six-foot unicycle or flaming

---

[53] This isn't to say insane spectacle wasn't already being employed in street performing. There's a legend, I believe in the 1980s, when a street performer in San Francisco secured several rental cars, with full insurance coverage, and parked them on the street by his performing spot. He then somehow got his hands on a mid-sized earth-mover and use it to completely destroy all the cars in front a stunned crowd. I can't imagine how this person could have possibly made their money back in passing the hat after renting all those cars, so I'm leaning toward this legend being pure fiction. But also, outstanding.

machetes, I killed. Not only were the Norwegians apparently transfixed by juggling in those days, but they tipped like drunks—probably, I suspect, because so many of them were drunk. I returned several times and made enough money to buy food, a few drinks—no small outlay of cash with Norway's super-taxed alcohol—and even a train ticket to Sweden.

Throwing Up – Professional Show Off 67

Juggling five clubs on Oslo's Karl Johan Gate

In London's Hyde Park, people tried to give me money when I was just out practicing in the middle of the grass.

On the other end of the spectrum was Las Ramblas in Barcelona. Back then this massive pedestrian street wasn't nearly the wall-to-wall musicians, living statues, puppet shows and all the rest you see today. How this spot even became a popular street performer destination I don't know. In the early- and mid-90s, few people even bothered to break their walking pace to watch me juggling my little heart out.

The few people that did stop didn't quite understand or didn't care about why there was a hat right in front of me filled with small notes and change. My first time on Las Ramblas, I juggled for two hours in the Spanish summer heat. Sweating profusely and probably heat stroking, I packed up and sat down to count my bounty only to find I'd barely earned enough change to buy a can of Coke.

I followed that up with a few low-key crowd gathering tactics, but Las Ramblas never generated enough money to make it worth the time and energy.

While experimenting and mostly disliking performing, the one thing that I did enjoy was teaching.

There is a decree in juggling stating that all jugglers, when asked, must be prepared to stop at any moment and teach someone to juggle. Any juggler caught denying a civilian a juggling lesson will be banished to practice exclusively on the Isle of Random Wind Gusts and No Flat Ground. This punishment usually isn't necessary, because it's a rare juggler that doesn't enjoy teaching[54] a new juggler.

Opportunities for teaching frequently presented themselves while I was trying to make it as a pro juggler. Schools, summer camps, corporate team-building exercises, attractive women walking by on campus, drunk people staggering by on campus and so forth. In addition to the excuse to take a break, teaching juggling usually results in quick gratification for both teacher and student.

Learning to juggle is like ordering a delivery self-improvement pizza. In 30 minutes or less, your student will usually be able to get six catches or more and, I don't care how old they are, work up a level of youthful glee that people don't often display in adulthood.

Sure, 19 out of 20 people will thank you, wander off and never practice again, or at least not seriously. But the juggling experience has been printed on their brains and, hopefully, a corresponding degree of enjoyment for it as well.

"Why didn't you become a full-time juggling teacher, Leif?" Alas, Juggling Instructor is one of those low-income, low-employment jobs that you do for the pure passion for the work, like a poet or ICE Agent. As much as I enjoy juggling, I enjoy paying my mortgage and occasionally eating in restaurants more.

---

[54] By which I mean "recruiting," while quietly whispering "One of us."

Throwing Up – Professional Show Off

I gave performing one last run in the mid-90s. Stories of not-so-skilled jugglers getting ridiculously well-paid jobs on cruise ships had gotten back to me and I wanted some of that payday.

The first step was to make a highlight reel[55] of my show to send to cruise ship talent bookers. In order to get the necessary raw footage for said highlight reel in short order, I entered the Minnesota Fringe Festival in 1996.

It was the third year of the Minnesota Fringe Festival, the first two being "quickly organized and under-publicized," and all evidence seemed to suggest no lessons had yet been learned from those experiences.

In 1996, they had made the encouraging decision to hire a PR guy. I mean, they *tried* to hire a PR guy. Instead, they hired what I presume was someone's college buddy to handle it on the cheap and thus no actual PR was performed.

To give you an idea of what we were dealing with, this guy organized a "media event," requiring all of the performers to burn a weekend afternoon doing five-minute excerpts of our acts in front of, we were assured, a room full of reporters and cameras. This plan had only one failing: No media attended. After some interrogation, it was revealed that no media had attended because no media had been invited. The discount PR guy seemed to be under the impression that if he just reserved a theater and called the

---

[55] Kids, you're not going to believe this, but to send videos to each other in the 1990s and before, we had to dub a VHS tape (Google it), causing a moderate to serious reduction in video quality, then mail it to them the old-timey way.

performance a "media event," the media would sense it over the media-dedicated channel of the Force and show up without any invitation or elaboration.

When it was pointed out there were no media in attendance, he didn't seem to grasp the cause, even after admitting he didn't send out invites. The good news is he had us perform anyway, for each other, so *we* could go around and tell people about all the acts in the festival. Even in the 1990s, PR bros could build careers by failing upward.

I ran around telling everyone I'd ever met to come see my show, not an easy endeavor since none of us had email. I did the 1996 equivalent of Facebooking the event by printing out my own posters[56] and stapling them to vertical surfaces all over Minneapolis.

Despite this heroic effort, I lost money on the whole operation. How'd that happen? Oh right, I forgot to mention the Minnesota Fringe Festival, then and now, charges performers to be in the festival![57] I grudgingly paid the fee because it was still a cheaper and faster way to get the necessary footage for my highlight reel than anything else available to me. The alternative would have been to pay/bribe/blackmail someone to accompany me to my infrequent paid shows and have them shoot video while I performed. It would have taken months to get enough footage, devoid of children and drunks shrieking over my patter, for me to throw a strong edit together.

---

[56] By which I mean I made about 100 copies at work.
[57] Taking advantage of artists has a long and storied tradition, folks.

I performed something like five shows in 10 days, usually to a mostly empty theater, and I got my highlight reel. But, as has been the case my entire life, I was just a few minutes too late to the cruise ship booking, bags-of-cash party. By now, every entertainer in the country was wise to the flourishing cruise ship performing scene. Bookers were drowning in thousands of tapes sent by people like me and we were still in the era of magicians and singers being at the top of the cruise ship performing arts wish list, so juggling slots were scarce. The jugglers who'd had the brains and connections to do what I had done a few years earlier were ensconced and my days of pulling down thousands of dollars, with zero on-ship expenses besides alcohol, to perform two shows a week never got off the ground.[58]

I pushed on for another year or so as a solo act, which sucked, then gave team juggling a try for a few years. This led to the first of several paid shows with the guy who later became the other half of Duck and Cover, Steve Birmingham.[59] But I never really enjoyed it. Juggling out in the hot sun for hours, being aggressively ignored by hundreds of people, or performing in a mostly empty carnival tent was a real drag. Also, the Duck and Cover shtick slowly evolved into an experimental, drop-prone, remarkably dangerous style of casual gym juggling. This was highly entertaining for other jugglers, but, due to the lack of

---

[58] I later learned that cruise ship life was so lonely and demoralizing that large portions of jugglers' weekly paychecks did in fact go into paying their bar tabs.
[59] Our full backstory is coming. Just wait.

fire and the consumption of orb-like fruit, ho-hum for civilians. We eventually down-shifted our act to focus on juggling for jugglers,[60] which pretty much meant the end of semi-easy, pride-swallowing money at carnivals, birthday parties and beer tent biker gang bashes.[61]

I retired from paid performing once again in the late 90s and that was the end of my days on stage.

Any stage.

For sure this time.

Period.

Or so I thought.

---

[60] Duck and Cover tag line: "They make the impossible routine, and the routine impossible."

[61] The biker gang actually turned out to be a very convivial audience, but a little forewarning would have been appreciated.

MONDO – It Means Big

"Double Flat Bounce" – Duration: 3.3 seconds
In the category of tricks that should never be performed on stage is this gem.

Steve collects two clubs in his right hand. Using a kind of reverse Frisbee throw, he gives these two clubs a high toss, with helicopter spins. The two clubs split in the air while traveling in my direction, hopefully not too far apart or too close, and both simultaneously flat bounce off the floor. After the bounce, while crouched down because the bounces are rarely very high, I need to be ready to catch these two clubs in any one of about a thousand different possible combinations of spins and flight directions.

Assuming they were catchable, and I actually caught them, I pop back up while making a self-throw to free my left hand, just in time for a leisurely 0.01 seconds to locate and catch the next incoming throw from Steve.

The narrative thread of the previous chapter forced me to shoot past one of my precious few enduring achievements in the juggling world. So, let's rewind back to 1989, when life was full of possibility and I could run an entire mile without dying.

Saying that my first ever juggling festival was the IJA in Baltimore wasn't entirely accurate. I got a small preview of the juggling festival vibe when, together with several

University of Minnesota Juggling Club accomplices, I helped stage the first ever MONDO Jugglefest, in the spring of 1989.

Though it's small in comparison to today's Minnesota juggling community, in 1989 there were a respectable number of jugglers living in the state. Taking into account the jugglers in Wisconsin and Iowa, it occurred to us that we could hold our own modest juggling festival at good ol' Peik Gym on campus[62] as a kind of amuse-bouche for the IJA a few months later. Festivals in Madison, Winnipeg and Iowa hadn't launched yet, so for a time we were the only game in the region.

With this encouragement, in only a few months of planning, we managed to arrange all the logistics and even do a bit of press for Minnesota's first juggling festival. The name "MONDO"[63] was designated to indicate it was frickin' huge, even though that wasn't true in the first couple years.

A rather impressive 80-something people showed up—and so did a couple of the local TV stations, which was far and away the top of the media pyramid in those days.

Lessons learned from MONDO '89 and Baltimore, we really went for it in 1990. It occurred to us that getting priceless clips of us juggling on TV *after* the festival wasn't doing us much good. Part of our mission was to lure non-jugglers to the festival who wanted to learn, so there needed

---
[62] MONDO has since moved to its long-time home at Concordia University in St Paul.
[63] Always in caps. Always.

to be some pre-festival buzz. Ideally this buzz would reach kids ages 8 to 18 and their parents. The kids would then nag and nag their parents to bring them so they could learn how to do all the cool stuff they saw on the TV. So, we started an annual media event the Wednesday before every MONDO, called "Fire and Ice."

I don't recall if I was organizing this from the beginning or if it was handed off to me soon after, but for many years this promotional event was my baby. I recruited area jugglers to drag their asses out of bed and show up ready to juggle outside Orchestra Hall in downtown Minneapolis at 6 a.m. We assembled this early in hopes of getting coverage on the morning news shows in their feel-good/WTF? segments as well as catching the eyes of people arriving downtown for work. After MONDO settled into an annual February time slot, the temperature at Fire and Ice was usually in the single digits. Mid-20s if we were lucky.

There happened to be an ice skating rink in front of Orchestra Hall. We brought torches, lit up, skidded out onto the ice in street shoes, juggled and smiled for the cameras and passing traffic, while the ever-changing wind blew flames back into our faces. Since insane people juggling fire in wretchedly cold temperatures on slick ice was an almost irresistible photo-op, we consistently attracted at least two of the morning shows and one photographer from a local newspaper. I upped the crazy ante by showing up each year in a Hawaiian shirt and shorts. The others, being more

Throwing Up – MONDO – It Means Big

sensible, usually wore that year's festival T-shirt over three or four base layers.[64]

Warming up for Fire and Ice, circa 1996. Note the Hawaiian shirt peeking out of my jacket. A few minutes later the sweatpants came off, revealing my shorts, the jacket was discarded and two hours of hypothermia flirtation would begin.

---

[64] One of the best ever MONDO shirts was the first year it coincided with Valentine's Day weekend. The design was a juggling club impaled through a heart, with the words "Valentine's Day Massacre" across the chest. MONDO was a little more frisky in the early years when it was primarily attended by adults. The following year, the MONDO shirt had an illustration of Atlas holding up the world, wearing nothing but a fig leaf. I was absent, but the back of the shirt for the 18th year said, "Finally Legal!" That would never fly with the suburban moms today. Unsurprisingly, there were A LOT of design ideas that had to be immediately discarded for the 30th MONDO, playing on the "XXX" Roman numeral.

Getting the word out before the festival was, as we hoped, extremely effective. And as word about the festival spread around the upper Midwest, more and more jugglers began arriving, traveling from farther and farther away.

There were a few legendary years, like when we hosted a regional yo-yo championship, that the number of attendees (and their parents) at MONDO exceeded even the IJA festival attendance. We were very proud.

MONDO was also my first serious experience performing for other jugglers. Each year there would be a "public show" during MONDO weekend, intended to entertain jugglers and civilians alike. But 70 percent of the audience was either jugglers or close friends and family of jugglers, perhaps the most supportive, encouraging crowd in the universe. Miss a trick four consecutive times? Jugglers don't care. They'll watch you biff a trick a dozen times and then go crazy when you finally land it.

So, while I wasn't exposing myself to a high school talent show level risk of possible public humiliation, it was still invaluable stage time to build experience, improve stage comfort and work out kinks that wouldn't fly with less forgiving audiences.

I debuted a bunch of wacky tricks on the MONDO stage, including the now somewhat common, but still awesome, trick of juggling three balls entirely behind my back, meaning totally blind.[65] These days, people do this

---

[65] It's possible someone else did it first unbeknownst to me, but by the time I got good enough to try it on stage, circa 1992-93, I'd been to a few

trick by flipping each ball across to the opposite forearm, where it rolls down the little ramp formed by their forearm and back, into their hand for them to flip it back again. My way was more badass.[66] I was throwing the balls up in the air and just letting them lightly brush my back, then freefall into my hands. This meant the throws had to be far more accurate and I had less certainty where they would land. Let's see the #KidsTheseDays try that!

As teased in an earlier footnote, in 2019, we held the 30th MONDO Jugglefest.[67] This fact, no matter how often I hear it, never fails to stagger me. You know how time seems to race by and how old you feel and when you see a friend's kid when they're like 3-years-old and then, what seems like maybe two years later, they're starting high school? Seeing the number 30 next to MONDO is far worse. I mean, I helped plan the *first one* and now we're at 30? How old am I, 90? Then why do I still feel 27? Screw you, time-space continuum.

I'm no longer involved in planning the festival, and Fire and Ice petered out many years ago. MONDO is now so big that there's no need to continuously shout it out to the juggling world every year. Apart from a mass-Facebook invite, it pretty much runs entirely on the momentum of

---

IJA festivals and several regional festivals and never seen another person try it, much less perform it.
[66] Some might argue "more idiotic."
[67] In 30 years, I've only missed four MONDOs, all of them during the years I was living abroad.

being reliably large and fun. I take great pride in what it's become.

These days I just show up and enjoy myself, watching the dizzying action in the main gym, passing clubs with Steve, coming alarmingly close to killing one or two kids who stray too close to our pattern and other cheap thrills.

Notice I didn't say "talk to a bunch of strangers, make new friends and have a gay old time." You see, my now not very secretive secret is that I have evolved into a low-energy, borderline debilitating introvert. I'd rather have a juggling club impaled into my heart than talk to more than, say, three strangers in a weekend. The problem with this is there are about 300 strangers at each MONDO; even more at IJA festivals.

How do I cope? Garbage bag full of weed. Actually, I just take lots of breaks and let Steve play interference. Fortunately, Steve will unselfconsciously talk to literally anyone, from a guy with no pants wearing the top half of a Fred Flintstone costume all the way to the Pope.

If necessary, with extreme effort, I can initiate a conversation with complete or partial strangers.[68] I might suffer a tiny stroke in the process, but I can do it. If someone approaches *me*, however, easing into conversation is a little more graceful; but only just.

You may be saying to yourself, "But Leif, didn't you just say that jugglers are 'the most supportive, encouraging

---

[68] There are people I've seen at like 10 MONDO festivals that I've never said "hello" to.

crowd in the universe'? If that's true, shouldn't it be super easy and chill to strike up a conversation?" Yes, yes I did say that and, no, it makes no difference. Don't talk to me about this paradox, talk to whoever invented cascading, involuntary behavioral disorders.

With that nugget of over-sharing in mind, how do I get on stage and act as the high energy, goofball half of the notorious Duck and Cover? Honestly, I'm not sure. I'm guessing pure adrenaline plays a role. Thankfully, I'm only required to do that once or twice a year.

Juggling Is Easy – and Incredibly Difficult

"The Kick" – Duration: 3.9 seconds

This is the trick that started it all. The wackiness of "The Kick" was what first steered Steve and me down the path that eventually led to the signature Duck and Cover style of club passing. In our less refined days, our style was described[69] as a combination of juggling and kung fu on a trampoline.

For The Kick, I collect two clubs in my right hand and simultaneously toss them, flat, but with a fraction of a helicopter spin, to Steve's right foot. The key here is that these clubs must travel that distance with almost zero separation.[70] If they split more than an inch or so while in the air, there's a strong likelihood they will land wrong and bounce around uselessly.

If all goes well, Steve catches both clubs on his right foot, stacked in a manner that, one beat later, will allow him to flip-kick them both back into the air at me. By now, the clubs have usually split or moved just enough that, while the trick is still possible, the kick can cause the clubs to move and spin in a lively fashion. I catch both clubs, sometimes quite dramatically, and we resume a standard six-club passing pattern.

---

[69] By me.
[70] What we refer to as "separation anxiety."

Juggling Is Easy – and Incredibly Difficult

As I discussed earlier, learning to juggle is easier than most people realize. In every room there's some sad sack who claims they could never learn, ever. They just *know* it's impossible for them, without even trying once.

First of all, that's just ridiculous. Humans can learn anything, whether it's the few minutes necessary to figure out a new app on their phone or the two decades it takes to become LeBron James. Or at least the last guy on the bench for the post-Jordan Chicago Bulls. In 35 years, I have never failed to coach anyone to at least six catches with a three ball cascade in less than an hour. Usually they get it in 30 minutes or less.

Having said that, it's also accurate to say juggling is one of the most, perhaps *the* most, difficult live performance arts. If an actor, dancer or musician makes a mistake, in most cases they can cover it up without the audience noticing. Or at the very worst, it's a split second recovery that only experts and co-performers will notice. If a juggler makes a mistake, the whole act stops to awkwardly chase down dropped objects.

What would other arts and disciplines look like if juggling error rules were applied? Imagine if every time a violinist made a mistake, their violin would go pin wheeling to the other side of the stage and they'd have to run and retrieve it before continuing. Or if every time a dancer made a teensy misstep, they and two other people crashed to the floor. Or if every time a singer missed a note, the entire song would stop, back up a few seconds and start again for another attempt?

To make matters worse, jugglers are in far greater jeopardy of making a mistake at any given moment than most other performers, because their margin for error ranges from slim to practically zero, and there's rarely a moment in their routines when they aren't doing something where a mistake can't be seen from the back row.

It gets even worse. A juggling act can have tens of thousands of throws and catches. Can you do something, anything, tens of thousands of times without error? Even with something as simple as walking, in the course of 40,000 steps you're bound to have a couple missteps, trips, off-balance moves or kick something.

One of the greatest elite jugglers in history, Albert Lucas, is said to have done a show with just two missed catches in 46,000 throws. This factoid is even more mind-boggling when you consider Lucas' act consisted of tricks like seven rings, four and five tennis rackets and a combination trick where he spun two rings on one leg, balanced a ball on a mouth-stick, and juggled nine rings—while *ice skating*.

In some cases, on top of all that, there are external factors the juggler can't control that can defeat them, such as stage lights, sun, wind, ambient noise, peripheral movement, shouting drunken idiots, and ground stability in the case of jugglers who perform on cruise ships or a bad day in San Francisco.

This is a drawn-out way of illustrating that a perfect, drop-less juggling act is virtually impossible. In 35 years, I can only think of two fluke juggling performances I've seen where there were no drops—two out of hundreds of performances by some of the best jugglers on the planet.

Still unconvinced? Let's hear from some nerds.

The late Claude E. Shannon, of the Massachusetts Institute of Technology, developed a killjoy theorem for a three-ball cascade,[71] which presumably gets quite thrilling, mathematically speaking, when it's applied to five, six, and seven or more balls. However, I'll spare you that excitement and just explain human juggling limitations in Standard Leif Terms.[72]

Quite simply, human physical limitations and imperfections are constants in every performance for elite jugglers. For example, juggling with very high throws gives you a whole bunch of space to work with, allowing for all manner of wildly creative tricks or large numbers of objects. The downside is that for every foot higher you throw something in the air, the accuracy of your throw must increase exponentially. As Peter J. Beek and Arthur Lewbel put it in their tightly named piece "Studying the ability to toss and catch balls and rings provides insight into human

---

[71] If you must know, it's $(F+D)H=(V+D)N$, where F is the time a ball spends in the air, D is the time a ball spends in a hand, V is the time a hand is vacant, N is the number of balls juggled, and H is the number of hands, nerd.

[72] A crutch I shall lean on a few times in this book, so your mind doesn't wander to what's for dinner or porn.

coordination, robotics and mathematics," which appeared in *Scientific American* in 1995:

"For throws of only a few meters, a deviation of just two or three degrees in the toss can cause an error in the landing location of 30 centimeters[73] or more." Keep in mind, that's two or three degrees in any direction on the physical compass; left, right, in front and, most disastrously, behind.

Oh, it gets worse. Physics, after gravity, is a juggler's chief nemesis. What I'm referring to here is throwing objects higher to buy, say, two seconds instead of one second of time isn't as straightforward as it seems. As Jack Kalvan and, again, the prolific Arthur Lewbel explain in "When Balls Collide: Understanding the Skill of Juggling," full of enough diagrams and formulae to please the most discriminating nerds, if you want to buy yourself twice as much time to do a trick underneath a thrown object, you need to throw that object four times as high!

The reason for this cruelty involves some jibba-jabba about initial velocity, a formula that, trust me, you'll comfortably survive the remainder of this mortal coil without having to listen to or comprehend. I'll just summarize it in Standard Leif Terms:

Let's say you're juggling three balls and you need to get rid of one ball for one second to do a sweet trick. In order to do that trick, you need to throw a ball about 3 and 1/2 feet (or just over one meter) into the air.[74] If you want to carve out two seconds to do an even sweeter trick, you need to

---
[73] Just a hair under one foot.

Juggling Is Easy – and Incredibly Difficult

throw a ball 14 feet (four meters) into the air. And if you want three seconds, the ball must sail about 33 feet (over 10 meters) into the air. At that height, the throwing accuracy necessary to keep a steady three ball cascade going is virtually impossible without darting back and forth to collect each ball thrown a fraction of a degree off course. And this assumes you're even strong enough to maintain such a high pattern in the first place.[75]

Using myself as an example, again, studying videos of me juggling seven balls, my throws are roughly six feet high (or about 1.8 meters). The average wingspan of an adult male is a bit over two inches longer than his height. In my case (height: 5'-8"), when I'm juggling seven balls, I can only get away with throwing a ball about two degrees off target[76] before I get in serious pattern decaying trouble (best case scenario) or complete pattern failure and a brief hail of balls hitting the ground (worst case). Again, that's *one single ball* off target by *two degrees* while doing approximately four catches and throws per second. Letting that information sink in makes me wonder how I've ever pulled it off.

---

[74] For the nerds, before you start sending me lab-environment calculations to the third decimal place, I've taken the liberty of rounding these time and height estimates to whole-ish numbers, because I don't want my readers drowning in math. Jack and Arthur did that work, though, so buy their book!
[75] Spoiler alert: Most of us aren't.
[76] This stat was helpfully provided in Jack and Arthur's "When Balls Collide."

Lewbel and Beek helpfully continue on their raging downer, squashing confidence for both jugglers and aspiring jugglers alike:

> "Defining the physical and temporal constraints is one aspect of juggling analysis. A realistic model must also incorporate at least three other complicating factors. First, the oscillation of a juggling hand is not uniform, because the hand is filled with a ball during part of its trajectory and empty during the remaining part. Second, the movements of both hands are affected by the physical demands of accurate throwing and catching. Third, the timing between the hands is based on a combination of vision, feel and memory."

In Standard Leif Terms, what they're saying is no matter what caliber of juggler you are or how long you've been doing a given trick or pattern, these dizzying variables mean no two throws are ever exactly alike. In effect, jugglers are improvising every single catch and throw, even with simple tricks that they've been performing for decades. Of course, this is also true for baseball pitchers, football quarterbacks and basketball players when shooting, but those overpaid wusses don't do their thing four times every second. Get your shit together and sign some jugglers as spokespeople, Nike.

And we haven't factored in the combination of strength and endurance necessary to maintain those hyper-accurate high throws while your arms steadily fatigue.

Now that we've thoroughly established that high throws are fantastically difficult, you may be thinking the obvious secret to being a black belt juggling sensei is to stick to low throws, right? Bad news: While low throws are easier in terms of accuracy, not to mention less physically demanding, they also leave very little space to work with. Low throws also mean pattern speed must increase. This results in a rapid reduction of the dwell time of an object in one's hand between a catch and a throw. The lower the dwell time, the less time one has to correct for any errors from the previous throw and get that object back in the air with, ideally, a more accurate throw. And this reduction in time to correct mistakes means anything beyond a micro mistake will be the end of your pattern.

The point is, low throws mean you can only juggle three or four objects (five if you're really revving). There's scant time and space for tricks, while increasing the likelihood of collisions. Also, low throws are almost entirely out of the question for performers, anyway. People sitting in a theater, auditorium or even beyond the third row at a Renaissance Festival show need high throws to appreciate what's going on. Unless you're doing David Blaine-style, close-up street juggling, low throws are out of the question.

Unbelievably, jugglers found a way to make juggling even more geeky in the late 1980s. The story goes that three different jugglers working independently somehow almost simultaneously arrived at a juggling notation method known today as "siteswap," which allows jugglers to communicate patterns[77] to one another on paper using (are you sitting down?) math. Today's jugglers share new patterns and tricks using a method called "record the trick/pattern on their phone and post it on YouTube." The latter method has proven to be extremely popular.

Nevertheless, so you can fully appreciate how hopelessly un-datable jugglers used to be, and still are in some instances, I'll do my best to explain siteswap in a suitably engaging and brief manner that won't make you regret buying this book.

In its basic form, using siteswap is only boring, not baffling. Each throw has a designated number based on how high it's tossed. In an unprecedented moment of geeks employing normal human intuitiveness, it was decided that the number '3' would denote a toss in a standard three-ball pattern. The same goes for '4,' '5,' '6,' '7' and so on. So, a standard three-ball pattern in siteswap notation would simply be 333 and a four-ball pattern would be 4444, etc. That's how a siteswap dummy like me would write it, anyway. Standard patterns with no special throws or deviation can also simply be notated with '3' or '4.' Furthermore, the average of all the numbers in a notation string indicates the number of balls in the pattern. So, '7777777,' '7' and '86' are all seven ball patterns.

---

[77] Notice I said "patterns," not tricks. We'll get to that in a second.

Since patterns with an odd number of objects cross through the middle[78] and patterns with an even number of objects often do not (thrown and caught with the same hand, ideally in a tall, narrow 'o' pattern), you automatically know if a toss goes across the pattern or straight up depending on if the number is odd or even. Since we also know the relative height of each throw, we know how long before that ball is caught and thrown again: three beats for a '3,' four beats for a '4' and so on.

What about tricks, you ask? Well, tricks are not a component of siteswap, just patterns (which, yes, are also considered tricks, but they're sustained tricks, not a single-beat, one-off). But if you're the fancy type, there's no rule against incorporating tricks into siteswap patterns where time allows. For example, there are many ways to enliven boring ol' 333 with over the top throws, under the hands throws and so forth. Or, if there's a siteswap pattern that's 336, that higher 6 throw gives you time to execute a trick, like behind the back, under the leg or a hand-across using your mouth as a transition spot for that filthy beanbag, if you don't mind the occasional bout of E. coli.

There are also siteswap rules for holding a ball for a beat, passing a ball from hand-to-hand under a pattern, signaling a moment when a hand is empty and indicating if

---

[78] The sideways figure eight we discussed earlier, meaning each ball comes into contact with both hands at least once on its way through a full rotation of the pattern.

one hand is throwing bunches[79] of two or three (or more) balls at the same time.

You're gonna want to put down any hot liquids or babies you may be holding for this next part, because it's about to get cray. Whether you're interpreting a pattern you know into siteswap notation or trying to invent a new, untested pattern on paper, there's an equation to make sure what you've written is possible without collisions. First, take all the numbers in the pattern string (one rotation in the pattern) and add '0' to the first number, '1' to the second number, '2' to the third number, '3' to the fourth number and on and on. Then divide each number by the amount of the numbers in the string. The remainders must all be different numbers. If there are two of the same number in the remainders, your pattern is doomed.

That was a bit much to absorb if you're reading this while drinking straight grain alcohol, as you should be, so let's run an example to add clarity. When 0, 1 and 2 are added to the pattern string 3, 3, 5, the results are 3, 4, 7. When each number is divided by 3 (the number of throws in the string), the remainders are 0, 1 and 1. So, this pattern will not work, because the second and third ball will collide, assuming you haven't cheated and thrown the second ball a little lower to avoid the third just to irritate me.

---

[79] A.K.A. "multiplex."

Juggling Is Easy – and Incredibly Difficult

Now, add 0, 1 and 2 to the string 3, 3, 6, the result is 3, 4, 8. Divide each number by 3 and the remainders are 0, 1 and 2. This pattern will work. Math! Hell yeah![80]

Now here's some homework: is the siteswap string of a 722520 pattern possible?

And if you really hate yourself, try to imagine using siteswap for multiple people passing clubs together. Goodbye, sanity!

If all the mental effort illustrated above for such a plainly physical activity is making your brain hurt, I have good news.

---

[80] I'm just kidding. Siteswap bores me to tears. Math too.

Let's Get Mental

"The Admiral Ackbar" – Duration: Single 2.7 seconds; Set of three: 6.5 seconds
Without breaking the six-club passing rhythm, Steve throws a flat, no-spin club to my right foot. Steve does an extra self-throw to buy me time as I trap the club under my foot on the ground, immobilizing it, then get my toe under it and flick it back up at Steve. We usually do this in sets of three.

    Get it? It's a trap!

What came first, really smart people who learned how to juggle or people who got really smart after learning to juggle? Trick question. The answer seems to be both. And we have science to prove the latter.

    It may have seemed like I was being more than a little hyperbolic earlier when I claimed juggling was one of the most demanding mental disciplines humans can do. Researchers at the University of Regensburg, Germany must have heard some pompous ass say the same thing back in the early 2000s and decided to get to the bottom of that nonsense.

    They started by drafting 24 civilians. They pulled 12 of them aside, scanned their brains using voxel-based morphometry, a technique which measures concentrations of brain tissue, patted them on the back, maybe handed them 500 soon-to-be worthless deutschmarks for their time and sent them home.

The other 12 were also scanned, but then they were handed three beanbags each and taught the basics of how to juggle. Then they were given a goal: They had three months to work their way up to keeping a three ball cascade going for at least 60 seconds.

After the three months were up, all 24 subjects were scanned again.[81] The control group showed no change in brain matter. No surprise there. But the scans of the 12 who had been juggling "…showed a transient and selective structural change in brain areas that are associated with the processing and storage of complex visual motion."[82] Additionally, the hippocampus[83], nucleus accumbens[84] and visual centers had increased in size by three to four percent. The jugglers had literally grown new gray matter and presumably had a pretty good time while they were doing it.

In a follow-up study at Oxford University, researchers discovered that novice jugglers who had practiced for 30 minutes a day for 6 weeks showed a six percent increase in white matter as well.[85]

---

[81] No word on whether or not all of them were successful at running a three-ball cascade for 60 seconds.
[82] i.e. The bilateral mid-temporal hMT/V5 areas and the left posterior intraparietal sulcus.
[83] Where the brain forms and processes memories.
[84] The brain's pleasure center.
[85] Specifically, a part of the parietal lobe, which helps connect what we see to how we move.

The Oxford study also concluded that whether you're an awesome juggler or just an OK juggler doesn't have any bearing on gray and white matter development. All that matters is that you juggle.

For those of you as far removed from high school biology as I am, a quick review in Standard Leif Terms: The brain's gray matter is responsible for computation and processing. The denser it is, the better it performs. The white matter are the nerve fibers connecting different parts of the brain, which carry information around the brain using electrical impulses. Naturally, the more of these nerve fibers there are, the better one's hand-eye coordination, focus, concentration, balance, peripheral vision and other motor skills become. In short, the jugglers had noticeably upgraded the parts of their brains that make them smarter, faster and more physically agile in only a few months.

Throwing Up – Let's Get Mental

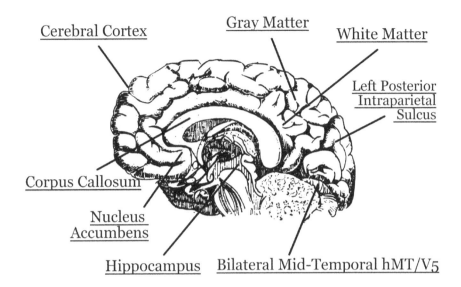

This diagram is approximate and my best effort. Brains are more complicated than you'd think.

Studies have been conducted with musicians showing similar results, though without the same degree of brain development. The key difference was that the musicians who showed more gray matter development compared to non-musicians had learned their discipline as children, while the brain is still capable of improvement, not as adults as with the jugglers.

It was eventually concluded that the brain likely responds positively, if not noticeably, to virtually any activity, particularly new skills like learning a new language. There's also a possibility the same may be true for familiar activities, like lifting a cider to your lips or picking your nose. But for the moment, juggling is the only activity we know of that stimulates this kind of dramatic development long after our formative years have passed. But hey, go ahead and pick your nose for 30 minutes a day for three months and see where that gets you.

This was exciting news, even for non-jugglers, because it had long been assumed that the only things that caused the brain to change shape were aging, disease, divorce, alcohol, aspirin, concussions and other shitty things.[86] In other words, we formerly believed the only direction for brains to go after maturing was downhill. Now we have clear proof that it's possible to maintain and, more importantly, boost brain power without dubious cybernetic implants or whatever was injected into Scarlett Johansson in "Lucy."

According to one Dr. Arne May, of the University Medical Centre Hamburg-Eppendorf in Germany, speaking to Reuters news agency, the changes could have been caused by an increase in cell production or by changes in the connections between cells.[87] "I believe the challenge we face is… to be able to adapt and modulate this knowledge into disease management," said Dr. May.[88]

---

[86] So, if not for juggling, I might already be in a nursing home, watching eight hours of "The Price Is Right" and "Family Feud" every day.

[87] It may be a while before we know exactly what phenomena are occurring, as MRI is only an indirect way to view and measure brain structure. To know exactly what fizzling and popping is going on at the brain's molecular level, we'll have to invent an Extreme MRI or something.

It wasn't all good news. When they asked the new jugglers to stop practicing and scanned their brains again after an additional three months, they had lost 1 to 2 percent of their recently acquired gray matter. The question that still remains: is there a certain amount of juggling one has to do, say, 35 years for example, to make that new gray matter permanent or is the phenomenon always an "if you don't use it, you lose it" situation? The upside is, there was no reduction in the new white matter after the subjects stopped juggling. So, if you quit practicing you might get dumber, but you keep the heightened aptitude for killing aliens and robots while playing Halo.

The concept of juggling possibly combating degenerative brain disease inspired yet another study, this time with subjects around the age of 60, an age when pretty much everyone is suffering mental deterioration of some kind. Unsurprisingly, these folks had a harder time learning to juggle, due to the natural physical decline we all suffer. In this group, only about a quarter of the subjects were able to master a three-ball cascade. But, those who did enjoyed roughly the same degree of gray matter development as their younger counterparts. Ergo, old farts reap the same results from juggling as young people—arguably more so because they're old farts who would benefit more from reclaiming brain power.

---

[88] If your curiosity has been piqued and you want to read the lengthy, science-y mumbo-jumbo versions of what I've described here, just Google "juggling white/gray brain matter" and settle in for about three hours of reading.

I have some totally non-scientific thoughts on juggling's effect on brain function. Having put down my juggling props for years at a couple different stages in my life, I definitely noticed a change. It *felt* like I wasn't thinking as fast or as clearly. Multitasking became more difficult. And I actually became physically clumsier. Then, after starting to juggle again, there was a definite sensation that all these conditions improved. So, perhaps not *all* gray and white matter deteriorate when I'm not jugging, but it certainly felt like some of it got bored and left.

With this new information revealed, naturally someone decided to apply it to self-help. A place calling itself JuggleFit runs classes in New York, sells DVDs[89] and juggling props and offers live tutorials over Skype. The sales pitch on their website explains that juggling has all sorts of practical benefits, such as relieving stress, fighting off Alzheimer's disease,[90] sharpening concentration, increasing dexterity, warding off food cravings and assisting in the cessation of smoking.

I can assure you that the part about warding off food cravings is a crock. It's a rare day that I'm not constantly hungry, usually craving three things at once. And Steve's attempt to stop smoking a few years back didn't get very far.

---

[89] Google it, kids.
[90] As far as I can tell, this is just a theory, perhaps ambitiously based on Dr. May's comments, that no one has proven, or even studied, so take it with a tiny grain of salt.

However, that part about stress reduction is accurate. Well, usually. If you've seen a juggler having a bad day, you know there's only so much sucking a person can endure before frustration and rage neutralizes any potential stress relief. I've obliterated perfectly good props into dust particles on more than a few occasions after 30 minutes of not being about to hit a trick I've been able to do for 10 years. So, *that* part is stressful.

However, in general juggling causes one to focus themselves into a state of so-called "relaxed concentration." Juggling requires pretty much all your brain's processing power all the time, so it's impossible for your mind to wander or dwell on your stupid sibling, bullshit happening at work or the perfect comeback for that time someone dissed your T-shirt in 1997.[91] Of course, one can resist this state of relaxed concentration while juggling and think about sucky things, but that will almost always result in really bad juggling and then you have two things to be pissed off about, so it's not recommended.

There was a brief trend in the 1980s when elite athletes were learning how to juggle to relax and focus themselves before competition. It fell out of fashion like 20 minutes later in favor of sitting in a corner, blasting one's tunes through giant, over-the-ear headphones.

Since I'm throwing around dangerously unscientific conjecture based on casual observation, I'll share my theory

---

[91] No, *your* shirt is lame.

that long-time jugglers, meaning those with at least five years of hard practice under their belts, perceive the world going by at a markedly slower speed.

It can be argued that jugglers' extraordinary reflexes are mostly based on programmed instinct for specific actions. An example might be a particularly technical three-club routine that someone has been working on for so long, they not only look badass when things go well, but they've worked through the thousands of tiny variables that can go wrong innumerable times and are usually able to correct them without a drop. Those reflexes are based on situational familiarity and don't necessarily apply to random, real-world situations. However, as I discussed earlier, I'm of the mentality that long-term elite jugglers have also developed a measurable degree of general purpose pure speed and processing power that gives them an edge in everyday, spontaneous circumstances. The studies done so far on gray and white matter development through juggling appear to support my theory. It's this heightened state that makes the world around them, even brief moments, stretch on for what seems like ages. Or maybe it's just me.

In my case, this sensation has earned me the label of "impatient" with my non-juggler friends. Their lollygagging civilian brains can't relate to my never-ending plight, like when I'm standing behind someone at a food counter who, after they've been asked what they want, will pause contemplatively for what seems like a full 10 seconds before speaking.[92] Even if the person ordering knows what they want, in the time it takes for them to interrupt their conversation, look up from their phone or just snap out of whatever daydream they were lost in, my high-test synaptic connections have already raced through the entire range of emotions from "neutral" to "Spit it out, simpleton!"

One of the reasons I don't drive anymore is because the stress of other drivers' molasses-propelled decision-making and reaction times was going to give me a "stroaneurysm."[93] The time between a light turning green and actual motion of the cars ahead of me was like being in a parade organized by sleepy kittens. And this was before there was a smartphone in everyone's hands. These days, the time between the light turning green and movement must seem like an Orthodox wedding ceremony.

But this drama plays out in the pedestrian world as well. The time between elevator doors opening and people achieving forward motion and getting the hell out of my way is like having a baby that's just learned to crawl between me and a sandwich. The time it takes for a webpage to load after clicking a link is like watching a portrait being done by one of those people that paint holding the brush with their toes.

All day long I suffer through this inching, creeping, boring-as-hell passage of time, where it feels like I could

---

[92] Twenty seconds, if I'm hungry, which is always.
[93] A synchronized stroke and an aneurysm, which is a condition I conceived of because it will probably happen to me someday, so a term needed coining.

have done five things in the span it takes someone to do one. Or maybe I am just inordinately impatient.[94]

Circling back to my slow-mo perception of time hypothesis, seeing the world pass by at this speed, while often being rage fuel, also has many advantages. Dropped phones rarely hit the ground. I get to enjoy my host's adulation every time I save an expensive wine glass from hitting the floor after it's knocked off a table by a drunk. I can savor "oh shit" moments as they play out across a room, already foreseeing how they'll end, while other people are watching, but not yet comprehending. It's a rollercoaster of emotion, I tell you, and is probably to blame for me developing high blood pressure at an early age.

In fairness, I'll also mention that my theory goes against several sources in terms of average human reflexes, reaction time, the speed of neural signal travel based on visual stimuli and the potential upper limits of these factors with the meat wrappers nature has given us. According to some people, even the difference between an unusually slow person and a conditioned athlete in everyday situations isn't especially remarkable. Then again, I doubt those people have ever stood in the hot sun behind someone ordering at a food truck who hasn't quite decided what they want.

Until someone takes the time to assemble immutable facts that prove me wrong, I'll continue to collect and repeat supporting empirical evidence as debate ammunition against slower-functioning haters.

---

[94] But probably not.

Let's Get Physical

"Three-Club Multiplex to Single Bounce" – Duration: 3.8 seconds

Duck and Cover is best known for two things[95]: Three-club multiplex throws and club bouncing. It was only a matter of time before we combined the two.

I gather three clubs in my right hand and throw a standard, underhand three-club multiplex at Steve. But instead of catching all three, he just catches the bottom two out of the mid-air triangle I explained earlier and allows the top club to fall to the floor. If I've spun these clubs perfectly, that top club should flat bounce off the floor, up to where Steve can catch it and we resume a normal passing pattern.

Speaking of futility, there were a few weeks in 2015 when we tried to do this trick in two even more stoopid ways. The first was exactly as described above, but with a much less accurate three-club multiplex hatchet throw. Weeks later, it still only worked about 10 percent of the time, so we moved on.

But! Not before trying the same trick above, but with *all three* clubs bouncing off the floor before Steve caught them. Though we actually pulled it off a few times, we abandoned the trick, because it was insane, even for us. But we did spend a ridiculous amount of time, trying it over and

---

[95] Aside from futility.

over, until we got it on camera. It's buried in one of our juggling videos on YouTube.

Now that I've unpacked the dizzying mental advantages of both short and long term juggling, let's discuss the physical. I'll start by breaking down the benefits to the body that most people don't internalize while watching some lame guy juggle lame torches lamely at a Renaissance festival.

When I meet new people, particularly after they learn how old I am,[96] they will often scan me up and down, noting my disproportionately developed arms, shoulders and back, and say something like "You must spend a lot of time at the gym." If I'm not finalizing plans to run away from the scary stranger by this point, I will usually respond earnestly with "Not really. Actually, I'm a competitive juggler."

What happens next varies. Sometimes there are intelligent follow-up questions. Other times there's a pregnant pause while their brains audibly swirl, trying to process the words "competitive" and "juggler" right next to each other. And then there's the never disappointing drink-spitting, knee-slapping laughter.

Though many people don't buy it, the primary reason my body has hoarded above-waist muscle is my juggling regimen over the past 35 years. Once you get to intermediate juggling and beyond, depending on the tricks and patterns

---

[96] As noted earlier, I'm told I look remarkably young for my age. Thanks for the genes, mom and dad!

you're practicing, a certain amount of physical fitness becomes necessary.

I'm fortunate in that my body seems to naturally want to build muscle faster and in greater mass than the average person.[97] However, like any strenuous activity, if you don't use it, you lose it. This became markedly clear during the four years I was traveling the world, working as a nomadic travel writer, when I did almost no juggling. In the first year alone, I lost about 20 pounds (9.1 kilograms) of muscle, dropping from 165 pounds (74.8 kilograms) down to 145 pounds (65.8 kilograms). Though part of that weight loss was the thin layer of fat I was storing which melted away through the combination of walking all over European cities and cutting soft drinks out of my diet.[98]

But I'm just one metabolically blessed, possibly part alien guy. Does juggling boost the strength and mass of arm, shoulder and back muscles for everyone? Kinda. The obvious stipulation is that all bodies are different and respond to exercise in varying ways—visibly and otherwise. There's also the starting physical state to consider. For example, if you take up juggling as a wiry, tiny guy like I did, you're likely to see muscle-toning results faster than someone that's 40 pounds overweight.

---

[97] See previous footnote.

[98] Fun fact: Two years into being a nomad, after a rather punishing five months of travel in Southeast Asia during the hot season, ending with a bout of the flu, I came home weighing a skeletal 124 pounds (56.3 kilograms). I was briefly detained in Singapore's airport on my way to the U.S. because I didn't look enough like my passport photo. I ate like a million cheeseburgers during that visit home.

In any case, discernible evidence or not, elite-level juggling is surprisingly strenuous.[99] A juggler's peak performance years roughly correlate with sports like football, basketball, and tennis. You'll recall that the greatest living juggler, Anthony Gatto, threw in the towel at age 40, partly due to the physical strain his act was starting to have on his body. He certainly could have continued performing if physical limitations were his only issue,[100] but he would have likely had to eventually reduce the difficulty level and cut back on the relentless pace of his act, giving himself a breather or two.

On the topic of pain, jugglers may not be destroying their bodies in the same way as ballerinas, for example, but there's certainly a toll, which can begin at almost any age, depending on what punishing lunacy you undertake. The mild side of this is tendon and joint pain in the hands, "juggler's elbow,"[101] shoulder strains, and, of course, the many ways one can destroy their back. The juggling community is filled with back pain stories. It's not uncommon for jugglers to submit to regular chiropractor visits, acupuncture, and in some cases corrective surgery. Jugglers over the age of 28 buy Tylenol by the bushel.

As we age, naturally all of the above conditions become more prevalent, or permanent, usually requiring a change in style. Which is why, as you'll read later, heaving

---
[99] Saying this in public also elicits snickers from people, but keep reading.
[100] Some elite jugglers continue performing into their 60s and beyond.
[101] Essentially tennis elbow, but less impressive.

Throwing Up – Let's Get Physical

myself onto the world championships competition stage at the corporeally declining age of 44 earned me the footnote of being one of the oldest competitors ever.[102]

If you non-jugglers are skeptical about the stamina required for elite juggling, try this fun experiment that I invented just now: Find a relatively light object, like an empty glass bottle of anything. In fact, find two. Put one in each hand and shake them up and down, arms extended forward from the elbow, like you'd shake maracas. First do this at about 30-40 percent of your maximum intensity. Not too taxing, eh? Well, do it virtually non-stop for half an hour. How do you feel now? Stings a bit, doesn't it? That's roughly the energy expended during a three club or five-ball workout.

Now shake the bottles at about 90 percent of your maximum intensity. I'll go easy on you, you only have to do this for 10-second intervals, twice a minute for 20 minutes. Can you still feel your finger tips? That's a five club or seven ball workout for you, except if you were actually practicing this stuff you'd keep going for an hour or more. You can take short breaks here and there, but not too long because if your muscles cool down, and you're on the unsexy side of, say, age 30, your day's over.[103]

---

[102] Though, if my research hasn't failed me, *the* oldest person to appear on the competitions stage, as part of a large team mind you, therefore not carrying the bulk of the act on his shoulders, has me beat by about a decade.

[103] This obviously doesn't apply to #KidsTheseDays, because those little turds can get away with anything with their stupid, youth-powered, resilient bodies.

Just watching it happen, one can plainly see that juggling works your upper body, due to the constant, repetitive, sometimes high-stress arm movements. It's like walking for the arms, except way more badass. That said, depending on what kind of juggling you're doing, you may be working your fast-twitch muscles more than your slow-twitch muscles—or vice versa. If your fast-twitch muscles are getting more exercise, say while juggling nine balls, then you'll likely increase your muscle mass over time. If you're using your slow-twitch muscles more, like doing five-ball endurance runs, then the development you see will be more in muscle toning, as well as unseen slow-twitch muscle benefits like increased stamina and muscle oxygen capacity.

I suppose if one wanted to glean the maximum fitness benefits from juggling, like any exercise, they would vary their workouts so that both the slow- and fast-twitch muscles get used. I have not done that. My workouts in the 1990s revolved around developing fast-twitch muscles for the explosive strength it takes to juggle seven and nine balls for a few seconds. Since my slow-twitch muscles weren't getting used in juggling, or any other form of exercise, endurance juggling wears me out pretty fast. Not only have I not been focusing on developing stamina-friendly muscle fibers, but also, and this is based solely on theories other jugglers have offered, I believe swinging around the increased weight of my arms is playing a role in my rapid fatigue as well.

Why do I maintain the guns now that club passing, mainly a slow-twitch muscle activity, has constituted most of my juggling time for almost a decade? The answer, oddly, is that I'm lazy. The more muscle mass one has, the more calories they burn, even at rest. Since my muscle mass seems to be playing a part in keeping me from going pear-shaped, I maintain it, because the alternative is cardio, which is way more time consuming and tedious than lifting weights. I'd rather subject myself to 30 minutes of whimpering pain than hours of relentless discomfort.

Juggling works the core and legs too. While your arms are moving furiously, the rest of your body has important things to do like constant micro-stabilizing, maintaining balance while stationary and, when things get hectic, moving and reestablishing stabilization when you have to bring an errant prop back into the pattern after a wide throw. And there's the not insignificant amount of work it takes to bend over to pick up drops 157 times an hour.[104] So, while it doesn't work the entire body as vigorously as swimming or cross-country skiing, juggling is still effectively a full-body workout.

As an added bonus, all that new, weird movement is really good for the arm and shoulder joints. If you keep on juggling into your twilight years, it will help ward off the loss of mobility and those maddening injuries we get as we age

---

[104] Alternatively, you can save energy like I do and just kick the props at what's left of Steve's spleen.

from stupid things like tying your shoes or sitting funny while reading a fabulous book about an aging juggler.

Having now covered in detail all the mental and physical benefits one gets from consistent juggling, here's a concept I've spent an inordinate amount of time thinking about for 20ish years: Are jugglers as close to superhuman as our species is capable of (for now)?

Before I get into it, yes, I'm well aware that even so much as casually floating this theory stinks of runaway delusions of grandeur. Anyone who sits down in a room full of people and proceeds to explain why the thing they happen to be really good at is the pinnacle of human achievement would be rightly mocked. So, I will tread as carefully as I can here, using as many strong lines of reasoning as are available. Alas, no one has blocked off the time and funds necessary to do a deep dive into this topic using scientific methods. So for the time being, I'll have to rely on what we already know about juggling's effects on the brain, supported by personal testimonials and plainly observable evidence from untold hundreds of other jugglers.

If you're not skimming this book like some kind of slappy-face ingrate, you'll recall the previous chapter where we discussed how juggling literally builds both white and gray brain matter. Let's take a closer look at juggling's tendency to produce oh-so important white brain matter.

As the white matter nerve fibers multiply, the brain's processing speed increases concurrently. Since the only study done on this phenomenon was only over a three month period of novice juggling, we don't know if white matter continues growing for as long as jugglers practice.

Dr. Arne May, who led the study on juggling and gray matter, points out that his study "...suggests that learning a skill is more important than exercising what you are good at already – the brain wants to be puzzled and learn something new." This means that varying your routine, learning new tricks on occasion, may continuously grow new gray brain matter like rising bread, but white matter will (or may) only grow up to a certain point. And let's not rule out the possibility, for now, that new white matter still develops even when practicing the same stuff long term, but at such a slow pace that we haven't observed it—yet.

In either case, whether you're breaking new juggling barriers or just revisiting old ones for the rest of time, is there a point where the brain runs out of material or space[105] and white matter production maxes out? Or can humans keep packing more and more white matter into their brain pans for as long as they keep juggling? I think someone should research that, with a long-time juggling subject (like me), for a generous fee, of course. Because if the latter possibility is true, and I've been constantly building white matter for the better part of 35 years, my brain must have the density of gold.

I'll back away from that wishful thinking[106] and charge ahead with the assumption that dedicated, long-term

---
[105] Or whatever—I'm a juggler, not a doctor, Jim.

Throwing Up – Let's Get Physical

juggling, while developing new skills at a moderate pace, means ongoing proliferation of white matter. But, only up to a certain point, no matter how many years you juggle or how Gatto-like your skills become. As the hum of electrical impulses zap across the brain's denser and denser nerve fibers at the speed of, well, electricity, the body enjoys a number of slow, steady physical enhancements. Let's take a moment to review them in greater depth.

Hand-Eye Coordination

On the list of augmented white brain matter advantages, hand-eye coordination is probably the most demonstrable. A certain amount of base aptitude is going to affect the speed of one's progress and, undoubtedly, the eventual upper limits of their hand-eye development. With results varying from person to person, it'll probably be difficult to ever nail down a baseline, never mind establish a predictable chart of improvement. We'll leave that quandary to the alien overlords that eventually conquer Earth and study us in people zoos in their free time.

Whatever the case, there's no question that consistent and frequent juggling will eventually have a noticeable effect on one's coordination. What does superior coordination afford? Well, the obvious stuff, like improved skill and confidence with everyday tasks, say, cutting vegetables or

---

[106] Though, now I kinda want to find a head-only scale for poor-man's research.

flipping omelets.[107] It also produces increased natural aptitude for new/unfamiliar activities and sports.[108]

A recent personal example of this phenomenon is ping pong. Much to my girlfriend's irritation—she's a lifelong ping pong player—my reflexes and hand speed made me an almost instantly formidable opponent. It took me some time to get a handle on offensive strategy and shot accuracy, but I was an immediate pain-in-the-ass on defense, because it took heroic effort to get the ball past me. On top of that, the combination of my hug-the-table style, made possible by my hand speed, increased the overall pace of the game, which caused her to make more unforced errors than she normally would.

Though I'm open to suggestions, I have thus far not heard of, or not realized, any skills gleaned from other sports or activities that can cross over as significant, instant aptitude for new activities as well as juggling.[109]

Peripheral Vision

Super-enhanced peripheral vision is only slightly less demonstrable than hand-eye coordination. Over time, a juggler's peripheral vision not only gets wider, but also sharper and more useful. But because there are so many

---

[107] I am, incidentally, the Kevin Garnett of omelet flipping.
[108] Or just plain aptitude if you started out with negative 1,000 aptitude, like I did.
[109] Before CGI effects became so affordable and amazing, I was convinced that jugglers would be excellent action film doubles for practical stunts involving advanced dexterity, hand speed, reflexes and the like.

objects in motion, simply relying on a wider range of peripheral vision isn't enough input to get things done when advancing beyond novice-level juggling.

    I'll concede here that sports like basketball also improve peripheral vision moderately, if not remarkably. However, when juggling even just three objects, a problem presents itself that most other athletes don't have to deal with. Say a baseball or football is flying in a player's direction. The most important thing is they keep their eyes locked on that ball. The player might also be keeping tabs on a defender coming to steal the ball or steamroll them, but catching that ball, that single task, supersedes everything else.[110]

    Until someone invents bionic eyes that can move independently like a chameleon, and then third, forehead-implanted eye-technology advances far enough, it's physically impossible for jugglers to follow three balls simultaneously, never mind five, six, seven and so on.

    Instead, jugglers focus on a single, fixed point; usually the very top of whatever pattern they're doing. In doing this, the juggler only gets a split-second, clear snapshot of each ball as it reaches the top of its arc and starts to fall. Using that micron of information, with help from their peripheral vision, the juggler has to do the math—four times per second!—to determine where that ball will be when it

---

[110] Including self-preservation in the case of football. I'll never understand why anyone does that to themselves.

Throwing Up – Let's Get Physical

reaches hand level, a total blind spot, and make sure their hand is there and ready when it does.

Here's the rub: At some point, not far beyond novice-level skill, juggling requires you to hone perception and physical awareness of the blind spots outside of your already enhanced peripheral vision. The resulting ability isn't exactly Spidey sense, but it's tantalizingly close. Happily, someone has put a little work into studying this highly specific facet of juggling.

While a grad student at M.I.T. in 1974, a nerd named Howard A. Austin decided to test the limits of how much sight information a juggler needed to keep a three-ball cascade going, using jugglers of intermediate skill level.[111]

Austin put a "fanlike screen" in the area between jugglers' outstretched hands and their face. The fan had a wedge cut out at eye level. I don't have the exact details of how the experiment commenced, but Austin presumably started with the fan fairly low and kept raising it until the juggler no longer had enough visual information to maintain the pattern.

Austin was able to raise the fan until only one inch of the top of the three ball pattern was visible. That's about 50 milliseconds of viewing time,[112] according to his report. The conclusion here is that intermediate jugglers (and beyond)

---

[111] A no doubt wildly different measure from what's considered intermediate skill level today, but no one seems eager to recreate this experiment, so this is what we have to work with.

[112] For comparison, it takes a hummingbird a little over 10 milliseconds to beat its wings once.

only need a tiny bit of visual information to hold a three ball cascade together. The rest is done by feel, muscle memory and instinct.

As jugglers progress to expert and god-like levels of skill, it's safe to assume that this awareness and tracking of multiple, largely unseen objects expands to include most, if not all, of the area within the three axes of space around them. Most expert jugglers can execute tricks that require completely blind throws and catches or periods without looking at the pattern at all,[113] relying only on the sensory input of their hands and occasional flashes in their peripheral vision. Even completely blindfolded, maintaining a three ball cascade, at least for a short while, isn't much of a stretch for most expert jugglers.

One notable side effect of wider, sharper peripheral vision is that, even when I'm not juggling, my eyes are constantly dancing to identify every single object that enters my extra wide peripheral vision. I'm not sure exactly why this is, but my theory is that this has become instinctual over the years to make sure whatever the new object in my peripheral vision may be, it's not about to hit me in the head. I'm told this involuntary habit is really annoying for people with me out in public, because all that eye darting makes it seem like I'm not paying attention to whatever they're saying.

---

[113] A basic example: Most jugglers can watch TV while juggling three balls, relying solely on peripheral vision to keep the pattern moving.

Focus and Concentration

I'm going to group the development of focus and concentration together, as the differences in their meanings are academic.

These skills are more difficult to quantify and I don't have a lot of hard supporting evidence outside of that Oxford white brain matter study. I can tell you that, particularly as a younger man, I was able to draw on what was presumably superior focus and concentration in a number of areas. Before there were cell phones in everyone's pockets, it was necessary to either carry around an address book or commit dozens and dozens of phone numbers to memory. I was particularly good at the latter. I was also able to memorize scripts exceptionally quickly during my dalliances as an actor. And I was usually among the best in games requiring short-term memory recall.

Of course, there are many games and activities that require exceptional focus and concentration. Strategic games like chess, poker and every first-person shooter video game ever are good examples, though I'm not sure if I would rank any of these as needing the same or superior focus and concentration as juggling.

Balance

Balance is another story. For starters, there's gymnastics, unicycling, escaping from dragons across precipitous rock formation bridges with your ragtag group of heroic One Ring-hunting friends and a host of other activities that require a degree of balance far beyond what's needed for juggling. Also, I have always had terrible balance and 35 years of juggling hasn't improved it that much.

While it's debatable that juggling is the lead skills enhancer across all these individual attributes, I'm still not aware of any one sport or activity that develops *all* of them simultaneously on the scale that juggling does.

Sound reasonable? Am I kidding myself? Tell you what, write an Amazon review for this book, with a five-star rating, obviously, and let me know! Then have your friends and family all buy this book and write Amazon reviews, too. Keep going and going until I can retire. Thank you.

To close out this rambling, borderline dangerously self-congratulating chapter, let's talk about everyday applications for juggling-fueled, super-charged physical attributes.

Over the course of three decades, I have performed countless blur-of-motion snatches of objects out of thin air during accidental mid-plummet. These items have included pens, keys, food,[114] wine glasses, cellphones and anything else that might be knocked off a table or fumbled out of busy hands. In the instances when I've had witnesses, it's not uncommon to hear a combination gasp of startled amazement, caused by the near simultaneous realization that something is about to hit the ground and the speed at which it was rescued. In especially dramatic cases, I have

---
[114] Not always the smartest thing to snatch hastily.

even earned a wide-eyed "Damn, dude!" from people around me.

There are three identifiable components that transformed me into a prolific savior of falling stuff. The first is the programming over time that eventually becomes involuntary reflex that anything falling must be caught. The only instinct override here is if it's something dangerous enough that if you catch it, it'll kill you, like a window air conditioner, a lit acetylene torch or a boulder, in which case just let it go, man.

The second is the years of compounding training that result in quicker and more precise hand speed, again, something your brain and body will simultaneously program themselves to do over time. The previously discussed augmented white brain matter allows your hands to move faster, while the increased gray matter makes sure your hands get to the right spot to do whatever awesome thing you're intending to do.

Finally, the least verifiable factor (pure conjecture, if you'll recall), my belief that over time jugglers perceive, process and react to the world around them much faster than most people. In other words, jugglers see the world moving in slow(er) motion and are therefore better equipped to improvise actions that require split-second decision-making, coordination and reflexes.

Admittedly, all I have is Leif-only empirical evidence of my impatience with the world around me to support the latter supposition. And since I don't have vivid memories of what life was like as a non-juggler, I can't confidently say if impatience and brain processing speed are mutually reinforcing characteristics.

There's also a teensy possibility my ego is a disqualifying factor. You may remember my childhood wasn't exactly a cakewalk with my diminutive size, easy-to-mock name and so forth. In my late-teens, I finally started emerging from the mindset of being the smallest, weakest, least physically capable kid among my peers. This coincided with my growing juggling skills boosting my overall social standing and the slow realization that in some cases juggling was bestowing upon me extraordinary natural aptitude for other physical activities for the first time in my life.[115]

This poignant rush of self-confidence caused the needle on my ego-ometer to swing out of the green zone, somewhat dangerously deep into the orange zone for some time, something I need to occasionally check myself about to this day.

Peter Parker's transition to being Spider-Man without struggling with this ballooning ego attitude adjustment is perhaps the biggest suspension of disbelief leap in that entire story.

---

[115] I frequently entertained the fantasy that, with a few weeks of familiarization, I could be a half decent, very short, NBA point guard. This daydream was fueled by my ball handling, natural hand speed, seeing the world in slow(er) motion, my pseudo-Spidey sense and my ability to track multiple things at once via peripheral vision, aka "court vision" in basketball parlance. In (slight) validation of this 20-year-old delusion, there are now numerous YouTube videos that drill all the stuff I just described to improve players' court vision.

After this exhaustive explanation about how challenging, mentally and physically taxing, agonizingly difficult juggling becomes beyond novice stages, perhaps you can now understand how the years, nay decades, of juggling being a code word for clowns, geeks, losers and unwashed street performers has made me non-chill about the subject. Dangerously non-chill. It's gone beyond me becoming defensive when faced with these characterizations. I'm now in a place where anyone who looks at juggling and honestly believes it's a cute, rudimentary activity for people who couldn't do something more mature, I have to assume that person is a mouth-breathing idiot. The kind of person who requires patient assistance to get through everyday tasks and eagle-eyed chaperons at night so they don't get into a stranger's van or get lured into a street hustler's shell game.

As luck would have it, I have the quintessential real world example of such a galloping ding dong.

Go to Hell, David Hasselhoff
(And you too, Piers Morgan.)

"The Dancing Minnesotan" – Duration: 4.3 seconds
This would be a more difficult trick if Steve's spine hadn't mostly decalcified after a 30-year diet of cigarettes and Mountain Dew and is now as malleable as a shower hose.

Steve switches from a standard six-club passing pattern, throwing every club that touches his right hand to my left hand,[116] to a pattern called "ultimates," meaning he throws every club that touches *both* hands to my left hand. In order to make this pattern possible, we have to slow the pace a bit, but for the Dancing Minnesotan we have to slow the pace a lot because Steve is throwing every club to me from behind his back for six consecutive throws.

The fast body contortions and arm reaching movements to make this trick possible look like a very odd dance, where the feet never move. Ergo, the Dancing Minnesotan.

I believe it was George Bernard Shaw who said, "He who can, does. He who cannot, judges America's Got Talent."

---

[116] We old timers call this timing "everies," because you throw every club that touches your right hand to your partner, and it makes the most sense. #KidsTheseDays call it "two count," because they're not right in the head. (They're counting throws from both the right and left hands, so by that logic you're passing every second throw.) There are other club passing timing options where you pass every other club that touches your right hand to your partner or even every third club, which is the timing most people use when they're learning how to pass clubs.

Throwing Up – Go to Hell, David Hasselhoff

If the title weren't an immediate tip-off, this chapter is devoted to dragging notorious juggling hater, David "No, Really, I'm Qualified to Do This" Hasselhoff and his even less competent sidekick Piers "I'm Famous for Literally No Reason" Morgan.

If you haven't seen the show, with few exceptions, America's Got Talent (AGT) judges tend to be people who have washed out of whatever mediocre careers they might have had, are clinging to the bottom rung of show business and fame, have nothing else on their schedules and probably desperately need the money. This tenuous last gasp of their careers hasn't yet translated into any sense of humility or self-awareness, however. They believe they are somehow not only capable of judging the artistic merit of performing arts with which they have no experience, but they've also convinced themselves that they have authoritative opinions on the nuances of these disciplines.

Enter David Hasseljackoff. In his years as a "judge" on AGT, he famously spewed mindless opinions on the merits of juggling, none of which were accurate or fair. After a while, it became kind of a joke. "Uh oh, here's another juggler. Everybody stand back, Hasselhoff is going to crush this guy. This is great TV!"

For someone whose primary career achievements are playing a doctor in a soap opera,[117] playing second fiddle to a talking car and third fiddle to Pamela Anderson's right and

---

[117] In the acting community, this is considered to be only one tiny step above playing a corpse in terms of talent and respect.

left breasts, Hasselhoff's continued certainty in his talents and wisdom is an undergrad, abnormal psychology paper waiting to be written. Oh, and how could I forget he somehow found time in between these career highlights to find modest success performing single-celled pop music that mainly resonated in 1980s Germany, an era and music scene that shall go down in history as being about as dignified as the mullet.

However, the Hoff's timing is indisputably amazing. When he became the curious benefactor of a blip of Gen-X nostalgia popularity, he leaned into it and grabbed a job opportunity that was both high profile and didn't require any real work or skill. That particular gift has always eluded me, so kudos to him.

Armed with the unflinching, misplaced authority to assess live performance after having once done a little singing,[118] supplemented by what I imagine is a textbook case of the Dunning-Kruger Effect,[119] he convinced the America's Got Talent producers that he was qualified to play the role of junior varsity Simon Cowell.

---

[118] True story: The Hoff humbly declared that his song, the wincingly unlistenable "Looking for Freedom," was an "anthem" and "song of hope" that helped inspire East Germans to finally overthrow their communist overlords. Whether East Germans regarded the tune as a song of hope or a song that drove them to hope for access to better music under unification is unclear.

[119] Defined as "a cognitive bias wherein people of low ability suffer from illusory superiority, mistakenly assessing their cognitive ability as greater than it is." I'd quip that this condition would be easier to comprehend in casual conversation if it was renamed the "Hasselhoff Effect," but I think the "Trump Effect" has the lead on that honor.

During his tenure on AGT, JackHoff maligned some of the best jugglers in a generation, namely Vladik and Ivan Pecel. These criticisms usually revolved around how uninteresting their acts were. He seemed to view making four catches and throws per second while dancing and tumbling around a stage in front of hundreds of people as akin to scratching your ass and texting at the same time.

One notable exception to Hasselhoff's disregard for mind-bending physical achievement was when the legendary Passing Zone juggled three *people* during their semifinal performance in 2006. Hasselhoff was completely smitten. Though Piers Morgan, probably because he hadn't gotten enough screen time that night, felt compelled to toss out some half-assed, back-handed insults before grudgingly giving the duo a check mark to advance to the finals.

Yes, the Hoff wasn't the only nitwit judge on America's Got Talent—or even the nitwittiest judge. Pompous Piers Morgan didn't hesitate to lecture world-class jugglers on juggling. When a ball hit the floor during Vladik's semifinal performance in season 1,[120] Piers pretentiously declared "You even dropped a ball, which in my view is the ultimate crime for jugglers."

---

[120] As evidence of the limited information flowing from Piers Morgan's eyes to his brain, the ball was actually dropped by Vladik's assistant as he was tossing them into her collection pouch. The much older, and clearly sharper, Regis Philbin had to get up and point out to the simpleton/drunk/stoned Piers and Hasselhoof that the drop wasn't Vladik's fault.

Really Piers? Well, in *my* view, even one typo is the ultimate crime for journalists. I assume you've never made a typo in your entire life, because that would mean you're not talented enough to work in your field, right Piers?

It's important to point out that Piers, amazingly, has even fewer credentials for judging live performance than Hasselhoff, having never been in, or probably even watched, a variety show.

Also of note is that in 10 seasons of America's Got Talent, singers won the grand prize in five of them. I don't mean to devalue singing here, but I think this fact demonstrates the very narrow, stunted appreciation for the arts the so-called judges wielded. The non-singing winners were ventriloquists (twice), a dog circus act, a dance artist (who was, admittedly, wonderful) and a magician.

Alas, some of the blame for singers being judged more generously than everyone else belongs to the TV audience, whose votes also affected how far performers progressed on the show. Which brings me back to the cultural perception of juggling being mainly for clowns and guys in tights at Renaissance Festivals. This does not excuse Hasselhoff and Morgan from their withering view of jugglers. If one is entrusted to judge a talent contest, one should have a deeper understanding of performing arts skills than the average kid at a birthday party (that I performed at).

By the Numbers

"Three-Club Throw from Scissors" – Duration: 18 seconds

This is one of our newer tricks. We recently had a breakthrough on our success rate with this trick after letting it sit on the back burner for a couple years, because we'd prematurely concluded that it was prohibitively chaotic.

Unlike most of our tricks, this is fairly long, with plenty of build-up before the payoff. Steve starts by simultaneously dishing two vertical clubs together, with no spin,[121] to my right hand. I catch them simultaneously, sometimes with a little scoop motion if they've drifted apart, and stand ready to scissors catch the next incoming club using the two clubs in my right hand. Steve drops a single club onto his right foot and flip-kicks it at me, which I catch knob-side up in the scissors grip. Then he end-bounces a club off the floor to my right hand which I also catch in the scissors grip, behind the first one. Finally, he does a hatchet throw with a third club, which I also catch in the scissors.

With three clubs now dangling knob-side up in a scissors hold, I give the whole mess a small backward swing, then swing forward, releasing all three clubs. The tricky part here is I'm throwing three clubs simultaneously without actually touching the clubs, meaning I have minimal control over their spin, height or trajectories. The clubs hopefully fly

---

[121] A.K.A. a "static throw."

into Steve's general orbit and, with any luck, he catches them all, usually with a bit of accompanying drama, and we resume six-club passing.

One of the many individual areas of focus within juggling is numbers juggling, generally defined as juggling more than five objects. When I started juggling in the early-80s, five balls, five rings and particularly five clubs were stop-and-stare caliber tricks. We were so cute back then.

These days, if you want jugglers to even turn their heads in your direction when you're juggling large numbers of objects, you need to be doing at least seven balls (or perhaps eight balls depending on who else is in the room), eight rings or six clubs.

Some of you may be thinking, "Wait a minute, that's not a lot. This one time in college my buddy said he saw a guy at the park juggling like 15 balls." No, your buddy absolutely did not see that. I know this for a fact, because it has never happened in all of human history. Nor has anyone's buddy ever seen someone juggle 14, 13, 12, 11 or 10 balls in the park.[122]

---

[122] Never mind the strength necessary, in order to juggle 10, 11, 12, 13, 14 or 15 balls, one would have to make throws with no more than the following degrees of error: 10 balls = 0.67°, 11 balls = 0.89°, 12 balls = 0.43°, 13 balls = 0.66°, and we don't know for 14 and 15 balls, because it's probably effing impossible. These calculations were, again, found in "When Balls Collide." Note: odd numbered ball patterns are fractionally easier, in case you were wondering why the degrees of error numbers weren't chronologically decreasing as the number of objects increased.

Throwing Up – By the Numbers

Your buddy *may* have *ever so briefly* seen someone juggle nine balls,[123] if they somehow wandered into the gym where the world numbers juggling championships were being held. Or perhaps if sometime in the past decade that person went to college or lived near a health club where one of a handful of the planet's juggling gods practiced. That rules out 99.99998 percent of all the civilians reading this.

Now, there's a teensy, weensy, squeensy chance your buddy saw someone juggle eight balls for a few seconds,[124] maybe, but I'd bet 27 beers that person was actually juggling seven balls[125] (or fewer) which is the absolute upper limit for about 99 percent of all jugglers who have ever lived. Most jugglers are happy with five objects, particularly when performing for a crowd of people that can't immediately distinguish between five, six and seven objects anyway, so why risk the extra drops trying a stunt several orders of magnitude more difficult?

Why do so many people have a friend that thinks they saw someone juggle 15 balls that one time? Because their primitive, civilian brains could not process all those objects moving so quickly in such a small space. This is not meant to be an insult to your naïve, possibly high-at-the-time friend. Even experienced jugglers sometimes have to look twice to be sure how many objects someone else is throwing, particularly when seen from the side where all the objects

---

[123] Throws must be no more than within a 1.3° range of error.
[124] Throws having a relatively generous 1.1° range of error.
[125] As we already know, throws must be within a 2° range of error.

are whizzing up and down in a blurred, narrow plane of view.

It isn't until someone has been juggling for several years that their eyes and brains can process numbers of objects and degrees of difficulty with any accuracy. What largely makes this possible is hard-earned familiarity with levels of juggling difficulty.

The fact is, numbers juggling is only for a rare breed of borderline mentally ill jugglers. People who are comfortable with months of failure bookended by brief sparks of progress. People who are OK with the idea of working for years on a single trick when they could probably learn about 157 other tricks in the same time frame. People who have surrendered to having few, if any, numbers juggling compatriots and juggling alone in a corner of the gym while the rest of the juggling club engages in more social juggling activities. People who don't care they'll probably never be able to perform seven or more objects on stage anyway, because it's so hella difficult.

In short, numbers juggling is the vow-of-silence, near total pleasure-depriving, hermit-monk-living-in-a-cave-eating-grass version of juggling.

I spent about 10 years on numbers juggling.

I got into numbers juggling the same way many jugglers find themselves pouring extravagant time and energy into similarly insane endeavors. One day when I was eighteen, I tried seven balls just for a laugh and to my amazement I could *almost* do it. The next day I tried again and after 20 minutes, it became clear the success of the previous day was a fluke. Or was it? Maybe I just needed to give it a bit more time? The next thing I knew, 10 years had passed.

    Why 10 years? What was I doing all that time? Civilians or beginning jugglers, I'd like you to take a moment to consider how difficult you think it is to juggle seven, eight and nine balls. Got a sharp picture in your head? OK, now take that and multiply it by about 14 and that's how difficult it is to advance from six to seven objects, seven to eight and so on.

    Imagine you've indulged in a hilariously deluded and overconfident whiskey binge. Instead of resolving to drive straight through to Vegas with every friend and stranger in the room, leaving immediately because time is of the essence, you instead declared your intention to level-up the number of objects you can juggle. In both cases, when next-day you gets vertical, a number of regrets and hard truths flood your reality. In the case of the juggling objective, you'll soon realize that not only do you need to throw more objects (duh), but you have to do it faster and higher, using more strength (therefore tiring faster), with less space to operate in and less hand dwell time to do it all correctly.

    It's too bad it isn't possible to illustrate in easy-to-digest terms the amount of time, energy and sanity that goes into adding just one more object to your upper limit. If it were, I'm pretty sure most people would nod grimly, turn and walk away as if to say "You know what? I'm good. I'm gonna go over here and do something less insane."

That period in my juggling life is now just a blur of long stretches of failure, compounded by chronic shoulder and back pain. There were half-hearted attempts at physical therapy, stretching and weightlifting to relieve that pain. Roughly eight or 14 beanbags lost their lives when they exploded against hard surfaces during fits of rage. And the whole time, people around me were getting a whole lot better at a variety of less stupid pursuits, not to mention healthy interaction with other humans.

Why did I do it? Possible mental illness aside, remember when I talked about how researchers found that juggling three balls for a few months developed the nucleus accumbens (A.K.A. the pleasure center)? Now imagine juggling more than twice as many balls. Suffice to say, I left all but the shittiest juggling practices in a good mood.

In retrospect, knowing even in the midst of all those years of practicing that numbers juggling was a fool's errand with limited glory, I believe this drawn-out effort can be boiled down to a single purpose: chasing Zen.[126]

People go to great lengths to achieve Zen. Usually through religion, but also through meditation, cults, hilarious pseudo-science fads, drugs and so forth. I suppose a solid, effortless three ball cascade is the first hint that there's Zen embedded in juggling. I don't personally recall this sensation when I learned three balls, because I was a 12-

---

[126] Well, two if you count bragging rights.

year-old, Zen-immune idiot. However, little did I know that I was enjoying the state of "relaxed concentration" I spoke of earlier, which is definitely a component of Zen.

But I do remember experiencing several tantalizing keyhole-sized peeks at Zen while learning and improving at five balls. The first time I ran a solid pattern of seven balls, the door to Zen swung wide open. The first time I ran nine balls, I was in Zen's VIP lounge, wearing a silk robe, drinking an ice cold Pimm's Cup out of a golden, gem-encrusted chalice.

I just want to pause here for a second and marvel at the snowballing lunacy that drove me to learn how to juggle nine balls. I mean, NINE balls? Was that really necessary? In hindsight, it seems like the caliber of crazy akin to building a 5,000-square-foot, luxury bunker with five years of supplies for the zombie apocalypse—just in case. Practicing for a couple hours only once a week, there was no way I was ever going to be very good at nine balls, never mind show it off to civilians. I was like a dog chasing a car: I had almost no chance of catching the car and, if I did, I would have no idea what to do next.

Of course, more and more #KidsTheseDays are progressing to seven balls and beyond more quickly than people did in the late 1980s and early-90s. In 1980, it was estimated that fewer than 25 people in the entire U.S. could juggle seven objects for more than 25 catches. Today, worldwide, that number is estimated to be somewhere in four figures.

Why the sudden spike? For starters, nowadays you can set up your smartphone in the gym and video yourself practicing, then go back and study the video for bad habits and ways to tweak the pattern. Getting one's hands on decent video equipment in 1988 wasn't as easy. Also, there are now videos all over the internet of people juggling seven balls, which can be watched at super slow speed in order to study catches, throws, height, speed, hand motion, form and so forth. Finally, with jugglers starting younger and having new resources to work with, there are just a lot more people around that can do seven balls these days, which means it's easier to find someone to coach you through the maddening intricacies and pitfalls in person.

As you add objects to your juggling pattern, the speed and height of the pattern must also increase. As we've already discussed, adding speed or height (never mind speed *and* height) to a juggling pattern greatly increases the difficulty and likelihood of errors, which, inevitably, are usually accompanied by drops.

I've never been a proponent of this, but many people don't start out trying to full-on juggle a new, larger number of objects right out of the gate. They will start by trying to "flash" them.

A flash is when you throw all of the objects one rotation through the juggling pattern, then catch them all for a hard stop. So, for seven balls, that would be seven throws and seven catches, ideally in the correct-ish pattern. Flinging

Throwing Up – By the Numbers

seven balls randomly into the air does you no good, even if you manage to catch them all—which you won't.

Part of the mentality behind flashing a new, larger number of objects before juggling them is that getting patterns started when you're numbers juggling is, by far, the most difficult part of the learning process. Getting seven or more, let's say balls, transitioned from being bunched in your hands to being in a Zen-worthy pattern means seven ever so slightly different, but hyper-accurate throws to get the balls from whatever two, one or zero finger grip they're in up into the air.

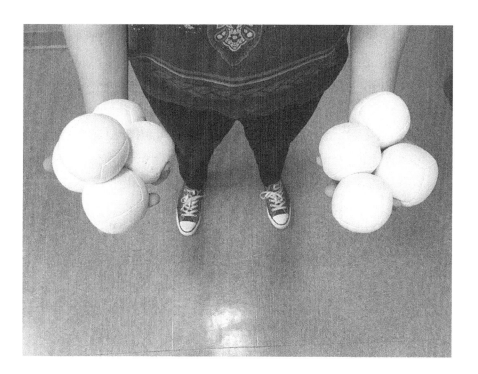

Throwing Up – By the Numbers

The typical grip for a nine ball start. As you can see, the only thing impossibler than juggling nine balls is starting and stopping nine balls without a drop when one's hands are this full. Photo by Sofia Noethe.

If it were possible to simply step into an already running, perfect seven ball pattern, one should theoretically have an easier time keeping it going, if ever so briefly. But of course this too requires extensive practice. And, if you intend to stop gracefully, collecting those final few balls in hands that are already at near maximum capacity is almost as difficult as starting.

A flash is not considered juggling. It's like a juggling preview. A "juggle," by definition, is all of the objects traveling through the pattern and being caught twice. So, for seven balls, that's a minimum of 14 successful throws and catches. After 14 catches, the juggle doesn't have to end cleanly. Hell, it can end with the balls scattered across a 50-foot radius, one of them in someone's drink for form's sake. You just need to get to 14 catches or beyond.

So, what's the record for juggling balls, rings and clubs? As of this writing, the records are as follows:

- Balls: 11 – Held by Alex Barron
- Rings: 10 – Held by Anthony Gatto
- Clubs: 8 - Held by both Anthony Gatto and Willy Colombaioni

---

The eternal question on everyone's minds, jugglers and civilians alike: What is the absolute upper limit of objects that humans can juggle?

Two things affect the human capacity for maximum objects juggled. Well, there are several things actually, but it can largely be boiled down to two things: Strength and physical space. There's also the staggering amount of training time it takes to add each successive object, but that's just a component of mastering the strength and physical space parts. Though people can progress faster these days than when I was trying to reinvent the wheel all by myself in the 80s and 90s, after a certain point you just can't get around the fact that you have to put in the hours. And hours. And hundreds, if not thousands of hours.

Strength, and by association hand speed, is a big factor limiting the maximum number of objects that can be juggled. It may not appear so from the comfort of not standing directly under that pattern, but the amount of strength it takes to throw all those little, seemingly feather-light balls or rings into the air is incredible. This is why many numbers jugglers often develop moderate to remarkably developed arm, shoulder and back muscles. The accompanying hand speed is necessary, because naturally, the more objects you're juggling the faster the pattern goes. And the faster the pattern goes, the less dwell time an object has in each hand between the catch and throw. The less dwell time there is, the less opportunity the juggler has to correct even tiny mistakes and get the ball back into the air with a catchable throw.

Once it became clear I wasn't strong and fast enough to maintain a seven-ball pattern beyond 14 catches, I started hitting the weights. The combination of weights and practice, after *many* months, eventually got me to the point where I could keep up with the speed of a seven-ball pattern (in those instances when I could keep it together beyond 14 catches, which was still rare). Working weights into my weekly routine became more or less permanent when I decided I was crazy-stupid enough to go for nine balls.

The second limitation to the absolute upper limit of numbers juggling is physical space. I'm mainly talking pattern width here, but at a certain number height becomes a limitation too. Humans can only throw so high, for so long and at such high speed before physics beats us.

At an as yet untested number of objects, human arm length limitations mean you can no longer make the pattern wide enough to maintain a viable pattern with all that stuff in the air.[127] Clubs take up the most space and rings the least.[128] You can certainly try to keep the pattern super skinny as you throw objects higher and higher, but that's when accuracy, and its downfalls, comes into play. The margin for error needed to keep adding objects to a skinny pattern quickly drops to near zero due to the inhuman

---

[127] There is, of course, the sliding variable of arm length from person-to-person. Keep reading.
[128] Never mind that the current world record for balls is one more than the world record for rings. These things happen.

precision required to maintain it. This is why horizontal space, and by association arm span, becomes unexpectedly important when trying to maintain a pattern at the upper echelons of numbers juggling. Also, you know what else helps numbers juggling quite a lot? Unusually large hands.[129]

Theoretically, the wing span of someone that's seven feet tall would potentially allow them to reach a larger upper limit of objects juggled than the much smaller wing span of someone that's 5'-5". This also holds true for relative accuracy of throws. While juggling nine balls, the seven footer has an advantage in that their wing span allows them to hold together a wider pattern, with throws that are slightly less accurate, versus that 5'-5" person whose smaller wing span, thus narrower pattern, would require almost impossibly accurate throws to keep nine balls moving.

Meanwhile, larger hands mean you can hold more balls and have a better chance of launching those balls accurately at the critical starting point. Large hands also mean there's physically more landing area for the balls, which can mean the difference between a catch (albeit probably not very clean) and a fingertip fumble.

An additional factor is environment. For instance, wind is a juggler's archnemesis, which is why you never see any numbers juggling competitions held outside. With the ceiling height required for the high end of numbers juggling, competitions tend to be held in gyms. The added advantage here it that gym lighting usually isn't blinding if you look

---

[129] Funny story: I'm not particularly blessed in either category.

straight at it, unlike the stupid sun, making life easier for the juggler.

With all that taken into account, where do we estimate humans will max out for numbers juggling? Alex Barron, the current balls world record holder, thinks that with the right physical attributes (strength, arm length) and enough dedicated juggling practice on this single objective (we're talking a decade at minimum, preferably without the distraction of a full time job, a significant social life or hobbies), it may be possible for someone to flash 15 balls someday. Maybe.

WTF is Combat Juggling?

"Between the Legs Bounce" – Duration: 1 second
Many of our tricks are dangerously stupid. This trick is just stupid, so we've confined it to the gym.

The thrower takes a single club, reaches back and throws it between their legs to the other passer, with both feet still planted on the ground, bouncing it off the floor. The throw must have lots of force, both down and forward, so that the club has enough speed to both bounce up high enough and reach the other person so they can catch it.

The problem is, this weird throwing angle means there's little room to toss that club with enough force to get the desired effect. And since a standard end bounce can't be done from that angle, unless you want to greatly increase the chances of the club bouncing straight up while it's still between your legs, you have to essentially slam the knob end on the ground in a hard, forward direction, creating a pin-wheeling effect that will cause the club to jump up into the other person's hand just as it's arriving.[130] If there's not enough downward force, the club is likely to just anticlimactically slide across the floor to the other person.

We can't take credit for this stupid, stupidly complicated trick. Another stupid trick aficionado showed it to us years ago and we started playing with it once in a

---

[130] Not enough forward force, again, may cause it to jump up into your testicles, or what have you.

Throwing Up – WTF Is Combat Juggling?

while, particularly when we're on floors with a gripping texture, so the clubs bounce better.

If you haven't seen it already, in 2015, a dramatically edited YouTube video made the rounds of jugglers playing team Combat at the World Juggling Federation. It was thoroughly mocked across the internet, even making its way onto the Colbert Report and Good Morning America.

But let's back up. WTF is Combat juggling and why is it a thing?

Combat is the gladiator battle of the juggling world. In its purest form, a game of Combat involves a battle royale group of players, though there are versions where it's one-on-one or the organized teams competition of viral YouTube fame.

In the group situation, everyone forms a circle, the more people the better. Each player will juggle three clubs, though there have been legendary games when some or all players would start with four or even five clubs, using the spares as missiles to strike from far away, if they aren't taken out first by a far more nimble three-club juggler. Players bang their clubs together rhythmically as everyone gets riled up into a (usually) simulated bloodlust, then on cue everyone begins to juggle.

A somewhat startling melee ensues—people running, clubs flying high and swinging at or near competitors, trying to make them drop—and it's every man and woman for themselves. When competitors are eliminated, they must

Throwing Up – WTF Is Combat Juggling?

quickly remove themselves from the playing area so as not to upset other battles. The last person juggling, wins.

A player is taken out in one of two ways; they are forced to drop or they stop juggling for whatever reason. There are myriad creative ways to accomplish this. The straightforward technique is to throw one of your clubs a little (or a lot) higher to buy yourself time, then use that time to flail one or both remaining clubs you're holding in your opponent's pattern. Your rival, if they're even a little experienced, will see this coming and also throw a high club in defense. This means not only is there no longer a pattern for the attacker to interfere with, but the attacker can also potentially be exposed to a counterattack from their rival, who will try to bat away their high thrown club as it falls. There is also the more difficult option of whacking a club right out of their hands, though you risk smashing their fingers or thumbs with this tactic, so out of courtesy it's usually not done.

There are several advanced moves that have low success rates, but are glorious to see when they do work. Take the "Brazen Pickpocket"[131] for example: A player will throw one of their own clubs out of reach, snatch a nearby opponent's club out of the air, or even their hand, leaving their opponent standing there with only two clubs as they watch their assailant's first club hit the floor prohibitively far away. However, this can easily backfire. If the attacker's

---

[131] I just invented that name. I have no idea what it's really called and it doesn't matter.

wayward thrown club hits the floor *before* they've stolen a club from an opponent, then *they* are the one left standing with only two clubs and a sheepish look.

There's also the even less effective but classic "Butterfly" move, when a player throws one club high and tries to interfere with two opponents' patterns simultaneously. The most bold form of this move is executed at a run, charging from a short distance away while throwing their first club several long strides ahead of themselves, thereby being too far out of reach for a counter attack when their club comes down. However, my favorite version of the Butterfly is the sneak attack method, executed the instant a new round begins. While everyone is still standing in a circle, the attacker throws their very first or second throw high and flaps their arms/clubs in both their neighbors' patterns before they've had a chance to take a step or even get their first three throws off. Combat is truly at its best when an attack is both cruel and hilarious.

Occasionally, players will simply wear down their opponents, either by continually launching threatening, but half-hearted attacks that their opponents have little choice but to defend, wearing them down and potentially causing an unforced drop. Or they will make their opponents chase *them* around the gym, until they commit an unforced drop or get so tired they can be easily picked off.

Sometimes both the attacker and their victim will drop while battling, meaning they're both out. C'est la vie. This is especially irksome when the attacker's move is more steamrolling their rival than an elegant club disarming, because there's no realistic defense against someone body checking you away from your own pattern. In tight battle situations, sometimes a hapless third person will get caught up in the chaos and also drop, even though they were minding their own business or dueling with someone else at the time.

If the predatory combatants get too focused on battling each other, they will sometimes all eliminate each other, leaving, for example, a nine-year-old kid that just learned how to juggle last week to win the round by simply staying out of the way. This result will sometimes elicit the loudest cheers, because who doesn't love an underdog? Such is the nature of Combat.

Most of the best Combat players will split the difference between aggression and fleeing, read the room and prevail through prudent strategy.

In one-on-one-Combat, competitors battle each other over several rounds, earning points for each win until the designated winning point total is reached.

There are a few variations in team Combat competition. Honestly, there's way too much to explain and, apart from YouTube highlight videos, you'll probably never see this version of Combat played anyway, so I'll save us all a few hundred words of reading. Also, you're welcome, trees.

Combat has gone through several evolutions. If you think it's hilarious/dangerous now, you should have been around in the late 80s. It was completely lawless. People were tackling and even high-kicking each other. Being that most people didn't get into juggling expecting to have faces smashed and knees hyper-extended, rules were quickly established to make the game more civilized.

But we were still in the era of super hard and heavy plastic clubs, so people still got hurt on a fairly regular basis and safety concerns began to grow. This pearl clutching peaked in the early 90s when someone at the IJA had an anxiety attack about possible insurance liabilities.[132] This led to a short, but ill-fated period of Combat being played with specially made foam-padded clubs. If I remember correctly, there was only one vendor making these clubs, and since we were all required to buy them in order to compete, that person probably got rich.

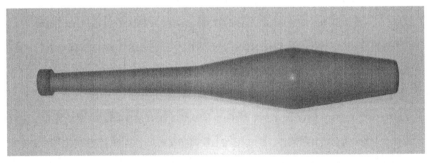

This photo of a remarkably well-preserved, early-90s foam combat club is courtesy of David Cain, curator at the Museum of Juggling History.

---

[132] Despite everyone at IJA festivals being required to sign an injury waiver before being allowed to step a toe in the gym.

The foam clubs did not hold up well. Chunks of foam flaked off the clubs rather quickly, revealing the wood and metal innards and rendering them just as, or even more, dangerous than playing with standard clubs. Some clubs didn't survive the six days of that festival, leading to complaints about having to constantly buy new foam clubs in order to play. As quickly as it was forced upon us, the foam club requirement to play Combat was rescinded.

I haven't played Combat since the mid-90s, partly because I was never particularly good at it, but mostly because I like the features of my face in their current contours. But it's a staple at most festivals and, it must be pointed out, rather thrilling entertainment, compared to baseball, football and those other sports where standing around is the primary activity.

There are several other juggling games, most of them with a lower nose-smash ratio.

Volleyclub is just volleyball, but with a juggling club. Teams can have two or more players, each holding two clubs. Whoever is serving holds three clubs, starts juggling, does two self-throws, then hurls a club over the net. A player must catch it, do two self-throws at the most (though one or zero self-throws are also acceptable), and then throw is back over the net.

Sounds pretty tame, right? Well, the club being thrown over the net can be thrown in pretty much whichever manner one pleases. This generally ranges from a gentle under-hand throw to a more aggressive over-hand throw. But if you really want to torment the other team, hypersonic spinning helicopter or propeller throws, or a wobbling, hair-raising mix of the two, will do the trick. In zero self-throw returns, one just bats the same thrown club right back over the net using the clubs in their hands. It's also possible to spike a club into your opponents' face in this manner.

Black Club, which has fallen out of fashion, but is still occasionally played, is like a more intimate version of vollyclub with no net. Two people pass six clubs with each other with one club being designated the "black club." Whenever it comes time to pass the black club to the other player, you can throw it in any manner you like, as long as it lands within reasonable catching distance. If the other player misses your wild black club throw, you get a point. If you throw the black club out of arm's reach, your opponent gets the point. If the black club is caught, there's no point awarded and the juggling continues until someone successfully makes their opponent drop the black club—and maybe two or three other clubs in the process for humiliation's sake.

Finally, I have only recently been exposed to a newish game that's essentially Bombardament with juggling. There are no teams in this version. It's simply a bunch of jugglers lining up opposite some sadist with several dozen of those rubber, nonlethal, elementary school gym balls. The sadist whips these balls at the jugglers in an attempt to get them to drop. The last person juggling wins.

There are, of course, many other games played with clubs and other props, but until a tightly edited video of one of *those* games goes viral around the internet, I'll leave it here for now.

Why Juggling Is More Exciting Than All the Sports

"Flat Bat of Doom" – Duration: 0.7 seconds
This is an oldie from way back in the days when Steve and I reaped more joy out of making the other one drop than successfully performing difficult tricks.

It's glorious in its brutal simplicity. In a standard six-club passing pattern, rather than do a self throw with the club in my left hand, I hold it horizontally over my right hand. The instant I release the horizontal club, I use the club in my right hand to whack the shit out of one end, so the club flies at Steve with a digit-severing propeller spin at something like 2,000 rpm. You can almost hear it cutting the air. To catch it, when he's crazy enough to try, Steve has to thrust his left hand into that whirling nightmare and hope he times it right so the handle (or the bulb end, we don't care) lands in his palm, before the club has a chance to smash the outside of his wrist.

There's a similar "trick" we called the "Buzz Saw," which is the same thing, but rather than give the club a sideways bat, I give it a forward-downward bat, so Steve has virtually no cross section view of the incoming spinning mayhem and, again, has to just stick his left hand in there and pray.

Back then, our practices were like playing Black Club, but with all six clubs being black clubs. God, I miss those years.

Is juggling more exciting than most pro sports? The short answer is "duh."

Having resolved that debate, I would nevertheless like to share my long-form opinions on these topics, considering that people like Hasselhoff and Morgan are out there spouting single-celled judgments on this most awesome of disciplines. I'm not claiming these are definitive opinions, or even fair.[133] Nonetheless, I want to get some things off my chest about the tragic under-appreciation the general public has for juggling compared to all the popular pro sports—which mostly suck.

Football

So much standing around, so little actual contact with the thing needed to score points. These are just two of my innumerable complaints about football. Some of these guys get more concussions per game than ball touches. And the sums of money flying around in this sport boggle the mind. For the cash Minneapolis recently committed to its new stadium, the city could have glammed up all the public schools to look like Starfleet Academy.

Here's an idea: Make it more like rugby, where play doesn't stop every three seconds for both teams to reset and

---
[133] But they are.

make plans to play golf the next morning.[134] Seriously, after all that practice, and for what they're earning, should huddles really be necessary? And for all the athletic reverence they receive, shouldn't these guys have the stamina to run and shove each other for more than a couple heartbeats without a breather?

Eliminate the huddles completely. Only stop play if the ball goes out of bounds or someone gets hurt *really* badly and, just for fun, add in a couple of snitches à la Quidditch in the Harry Potter books. Then a couple of guys on each team can just scurry around the field, seemingly grasping at thin air. That would make a great blooper highlight reel when they get steamrolled from behind by the people chasing the actual ball.

Perhaps this continuous play would cut down on the —I am not kidding here—*100 commercials* that air during the average televised NFL game. Holy fresh hell, no wonder the fans drink so much at these games. They need to feel *something*, because it sure ain't stimulation, in order to glean enjoyment out of this otherwise blindingly dull three-hour slog.

Basketball

Props to basketball for having longer periods of uninterrupted play and perhaps the highest level of

---

[134] You *know* this is happening in the huddle, especially late in a losing season.

athleticism in all the pro sports categories. My main problem is that guys are getting eight-figure salaries for a sport where 10 grown, fantastically athletic men play with *one* goddamn ball. One ball? Come on guys, that's way too much time with idle hands. With the speed and reflexes these guys have, they should be able to keep track of more than one ball at a time.

Put two balls in there. Or even five balls. Now *that* would be exciting. Think of the passing, the combo plays, the bait-and-switches and the see-sawing point totals leaving the fans breathless. Not to mention that it would make the announcers have to really work for a living. Talk about a cakewalk job. How do I get in on that?

Baseball

God, I hate baseball. When it comes to standing around, scratching one's genitals and spitting for no reason, there is no equal to baseball. Well, maybe cricket. The inching speed of baseball play should come as no surprise, as it was initially conceived of during the simpler, quaint mid-19th century, when traveling eight miles per hour on a bicycle was considered terrifying. In a typical game (three hours, 12 minutes) there is an average of 18 minutes of actual action. This stat never fails to blow my mind. Guys get paid ridiculous sums to *maybe* touch a ball once or twice in three hours and *maybe* hit a ball with a stick once every three or four games.

Which brings us to the confoundingly low expectations for batting. Batting .400 (successfully hitting the ball once every 2.5 tries into the playing field without it being caught before it hits the ground) is considered to be the apex of batting skill. Really? Toddlers can catch a bouncy ball with higher frequency! If a juggler only successfully executed their tricks 40 percent of the time, they'd be considered the worst juggler on the planet. No bumpkin, back-country carnival would let that kind of juggling show on their variety stage, even for free.

And yet, people pay good money to go to baseball games and, frankly, absurd money for terrible food and beer, just to see fleeting moments of action in the otherwise standstill 174 minutes of an average game.

Recognizing this ever-present threat of fan boredom, stadiums now attempt to fill every single lull in the game with some kind of mascot skit, T-shirt bazooka barrage, kiss cams pointed at siblings and coworkers and so forth. At least there's ample time to catch up with friends you haven't seen in years. In fact, baseball games would be the perfect place to hold high school reunions.

Tennis

Like basketball, tennis gets athleticism points for the potential for extended periods of action with only short breaks in between. But haven't we grown beyond two people swatting a ball back and forth, over a uniform height net, on a perfectly flat surface? Where's the thrill in that? I propose we string a net across a skateboard park and play on that crazy rolling, wavy, sometimes near-vertical area. Suddenly predicting where the ball will go gets, like, 20 times more difficult, and the potential for wacky trick shots also skyrockets. To account for this exciting randomness, we can allow up to two bounces on each side of the net before return. And every court should have different topography, to keep people on their toes. Would that be awesome or what?

Soccer

There are two key problems with soccer: Not enough scoring and the players are the biggest, most melodramatic babies in all of professional sports. Except for just a little bit in basketball, is there any other sport where pretending to be injured is part of a shrewd playing strategy that can lead to lucrative contracts and endorsement deals? And there are almost never any consequences for basically lying to the referees! Man up, play the damn game or GTFO.[135]

Golf

Do I really need to go into detail on the myriad, virtually endless ways juggling is superior to golf? I still can't believe this is considered a sport, never mind the sums of money one can earn strolling around, hitting a ball once every 20 minutes. And the guys that carry their own bags are lauded as some kind of badasses! Any activity where carrying 20

---

[135] I went with "man up" here, because for the most part women soccer players fall down for nothing less than a compound fracture.

pounds a mile, with something like 100 breaks, is considered a herculean effort really needs to reevaluate its definition of badass. Dude, I carry more than twice that weight eight blocks home from the grocery store every week. Where's my offer for a Cadillac commercial?

Cricket

All the action of baseball and the exhilaration of golf packed into a game that can last up to 30 hours. I'm still not 100 percent convinced this isn't an elaborate practical joke that got out of hand.

How I Became A Competitive Athlete at Age 44

"Two Club Multiplex Hatchet to a Partial Behind the Back Catch" – Duration: 2.3 seconds
I can't speak for Steve, since he catches this trick, but from my side, this trick is easy. And for some reason jugglers love it.

I gather two clubs in my right hand and throw a two-club multiplex hatchet throw at Steve. The only challenge with this throw is that the spin and height have a somewhat narrow margin of error, but not prohibitively so. When the two hatchet-throw clubs arrive, Steve catches them simultaneously, one normally with his left hand and the other with his right hand behind his back on the left side of his body.

It's only slightly more challenging that a single club behind the back catch, but the 'wooooo!'s we get from jugglers when we perform this are disproportionately loud, so I don't know what's going through their heads. They're jugglers, sitting in an audience at the end of a long day with no responsibility, so there's a better than average chance they're drunk.

By this point in the book, one thought that may have run through your mind a few times: "Come on, is juggling *really* a sport? It seems more like performance art—at best." There are wide-ranging opinions on the subject.

I plainly fall on the sport side of this debate. I've already gone into detail about how physically demanding elite juggling can be. Depending on which sub-discipline you choose, once you reach a certain stage you literally cannot progress without a degree of strength and stamina. Photographers, sculptors and painters don't get out of breath while they're working.[136] The same sports argument goes for almost all forms of dancing, too.

Also, my overdeveloped arms, shoulders and back aren't because I wail on my upper body two hours a day, five days a week at the gym. I lift weights for about 30 minutes twice a week, otherwise those muscles are built from juggling.

I could press on with my sports argument for another thousand words here, but I have a tale of heroism and stupidity to tell which will be long enough without getting bogged down in a mammoth digression. Instead, if you want to read 6,700 convincing words about how un-effing-believably difficult world-class juggling is, you should Google and absorb Jason Fagone's "Dropped," the story of the greatest juggler alive, Anthony Gatto, and his retirement at the age of 40.

One of the gems in Fagone's outstanding piece is this quote from the one and only Arthur Lewbel[137]:

---

[136] At least I hope not.

"You're making four throws a second. In a minute, you might have more throws and catches than an entire baseball game. So doing something for even a minute without a mistake is enormously hard—like a whole baseball game without an error."

And that's just basic three object juggling. Add in the compounding difficulty of tricks, or worse, more objects, think about the thousands of minuscule, ongoing corrections to compensate for throws that aren't perfect,[138] consider the near zero margin for error with some tricks, and juggling suddenly starts to resemble a genuine superpower. Like I said earlier, it's not quite Spider-Man caliber, but way more impressive than Hawkeye from The Avengers.

And for the record, four throws and catches per second for 60 seconds is 240 throws and catches, far more throws and catches than any baseball game I've ever seen.

As you may have noted in the title of this book, I have more than 35 sometimes sporadic years of juggling under my belt, with the intuitive and natural advantage of having learned as a kid. Included in that figure are several years when my practice time and dedication were practically zero, namely when I realized that high school sports were probably better for my social standing than juggling. I took another break for a few years during and after university while I was

---

[137] He of the book "When Balls Collide" and other previously noted science-y essays on juggling.
[138] Spoiler alert: Almost all of them.

embroiled in theater. I barely juggled at all during the four and a half years in my 30s while I was doing my nomadic wandering of the planet that led to my career in travel writing. But I was far beyond any serious juggling aspirations by that point. Or so I thought at the time.

At some stage in my mid-20s, I realized that I would never be a great juggler. Pretty good, yes, but not great. Not great enough to compete in the world championships. I had enviable aptitude, but I was not god-like and only god-like jugglers have a shot at a medal. Hell, some years the field of competitors is so wondrously dense, one needs to be god-like just to get into the competition and finish *last*.

I practiced hard, but probably not hard enough. And I wasn't focused. Rather than become exceptional at certain disciplines within juggling, I wanted to sample *all* of juggling —balls, rings, clubs, diabolo, devil sticks, cigar boxes, spinning balls, unicycle—including, as we learned earlier, frittering away half the 90s practicing numbers juggling.

More problematic to my competition aspirations were the double whammy affects of my lack of consistency and the amazing, almost unbelievable bad luck vibes I seemed to emanate while on stage. A prime example was the first ever "Canadian National Championships"[139] in Winnipeg in 1991. Naturally, a bunch of us Minnesotans drove up to compete

---

[139] There was no other entity claiming this title, so Winnipeg decided to just take it and run.

How I Became A Competitive Athlete at Age 44

in the hopes of nabbing the title away from an actual Canadian.[140]

I had a very solid, wide-ranging routine that involved a variety of props. As my competitors later told me, the flashy, creative first minute or so of my three club routine was an "oh shit" moment for everyone. Then all four wheels came off in classic Leif fashion. My props seemingly became sentient and unified into a kind of Avengers team, bent on embarrassing me at every opportunity.

My clubs would spin onto previously unknown/unseen trajectories and rotations, colliding in mid-air and exploding tens of feet in different directions, requiring a few moments of scurrying back and forth to retrieve them all. Balls that I'd cleanly caught would get knocked out of my hands and onto the floor by other balls. Clubs thrown high for a pirouette would be nowhere in sight after I stopped spinning, then crash to the floor several feet away or come a whisker away from breaking my nose.[141] Props that I threw to the side when I was done with them would hit the floor funny and roll back right into my way. It was an unmitigated disaster which my fellow competitors enjoyed immensely.

It was also around this period in time that I realized serious world-class juggling competition required near-Olympic caliber dedication and training hours and I had

---
[140] We didn't.
[141] It was about this time that I decided that pirouettes were stupid and lame and I never put them in my act again.

other things going on that I simply couldn't (or wouldn't) sacrifice, like school, earning a sustainable income and kissing girls. I abandoned my dreams of competing and steered onto a jugging path that held less potential for public humiliation.

Flash to New Year's Eve, 2012. While getting blitzed on cider at a small gathering with Steve, the idea was floated that we should make a run for the championships. More accurately, we were "Kramered" into it by Steve's girlfriend, who I've since concluded is a gifted sociopath.

Sensible people would have dismissed the idea immediately. We were both in our 40s, nearly double the age of most other competitors. We had jobs and other commitments that would affect how much we could train. We were both legendarily non-ambitious when it came to juggling. For most of the years I'd known him, outside of juggling for which he is tireless, Steve had the energy and self-starter motivation of a baby panda.

However, as I said, I was swimming in cider at the time (my sodium pentothal), meaning my weakness for flattery and susceptibility to suggestion was at puppy levels. Also, it was rightly pointed out that we had almost 25 years worth of gym time together already stockpiled, meaning we already had a considerable foundation of tricks to choose from and build on. Suddenly it didn't seem so crazy. Why, we could have a competition-worthy routine put together in a matter of weeks! No one has done crazy tricks like ours in competition before. Those judges won't know what hit them! Hey, pour me s'more cider, will you? Actually, just give me the bottle.

We resolved to go for it—for the fans.

Yes, even sober it was accurate to say we had fans. Probably only tens of fans, but fans nonetheless, mainly composed of club passing enthusiasts. Steve and I had quietly developed into something of a novelty duo over the years, doing wackadoodle six-club passing tricks no one had seen before, that pushed the boundaries of what was realistic and sane. We dreamed up and practiced tricks that only lunatics, masochists and the highly delusional would consider. Tricks where significant injuries were a constant possibility. We were a danger to ourselves—and others. At the Monday night juggling club meetings in South Minneapolis, with our reputation for unpredictability and (purely accidental) violence, Steve and I had about 1/4 of the room entirely to ourselves at one particularly treacherous stage in our development. Our premeditated chaos, and the zone it encompassed, was amplified by the fact that we didn't necessary view dropping as a bad thing.

In the Duck and Cover mindset, drops weren't drops so much as they were opportunities to improvise another trick. Any club that hit the ground, but was still bouncing or rolling within reach was fair game to be batted, kicked or generally flailed at to get it back in the air and into the other person's orbit, at which point it became their problem. The constant action and creative, split-second improvisation of our practices was exhilarating.

Unfortunately, this go-for-broke instinct occasionally resulted in a club flying high and way outside our catching radius with something like a quintuple rotation helicopter spin on it. Anyone that strayed too close to us while we were practicing was quickly reminded about the ear-ringing pain of a direct head-shot with a club. Now we were planning to take this unorthodox style and general indifference to drops and hone it into a championship routine.

In the harsh light of sobriety we didn't change our minds, but we agreed that realistically it was unlikely that we would win. At best we'd blow the backs off a lot of people's heads and that was good enough for us. We decided simply earning a medal was our goal. But first, we had an even more modest goal.

If we were going to get past the preliminary championship auditions, our first order of business was the considerable work needed to improve our consistency. Some of our tricks were so sensitive and precise that the moon's orbit was probably affecting our ability to pull them off on certain days. With the staggering amount of practice we needed to rein in that unpredictability and not embarrass ourselves in a hail of drops or injuries requiring on-stage medical attention, we wisely decided to not compete that upcoming summer, but rather aim for summer 2014. That gave us about 15 months to get our act together.

The huge training lead time was also out of respect for our ages and physical limits. Competitive juggling, like many physical sports, doesn't see many old timers. It's mainly an arena for people in their late teens and early 20s. By their late 20s, competitive jugglers start slowing down, either due to the punishing physical demands or, more often, Real Life asserts itself and they just don't have the time to train for competition with the distraction of jobs and families and so forth.

Once in a while someone in their 30s will compete and on rare occasions over the years, one or two individuals in their 40s or older have clambered onto the stage, usually playing a minor role on teams of four or more people. I would be competing for the world championships on a two-person team, in one of the most all around demanding activities known to man, at the age of 44.

We started training in earnest in April 2013. We needed a conveniently located training space that we could access seven days a week, so we got a dual, "family" membership at the downtown Minneapolis YMCA.[142]

Like so many jugglers before us, we practiced in the racquetball courts, both for the high ceilings and so we didn't concuss the people on the cardio machines when things got out of hand. The downside was that the wicked echo in those things made conversation from more than a

---

[142] If anyone asks, we're life partners.

few feet away nearly impossible. Steve and I were like an old couple in there.

"I need a bit more time for this trick. Throw that club higher!"

"What??"

"I said, throw that club higher!!"

"No thanks, I ate before I came here."

The first setback presented itself after only a few days. Our creaky bodies weren't prepared for a sudden increase in practice time. Though we were both relatively spry for our ages (I was 42 and Steve was 40 at the time) even after decades of juggling muscle memory and conditioning, we weren't physically prepared for the transition from lazy goofing off once a week to intense training four or five days a week.

Within days our arms, shoulders and backs were alive with pain. I was even limping at one stage for some reason. We scaled back our training hours to allow our bodies to adjust for the quiet physical decline that had begun unbeknownst to us.

Though our bodies adjusted over time, it never got easy. In order to coax my arms, shoulders and back into peak condition, I rededicated myself to twice-weekly weight lifting. When the rest of my body started complaining, I began to go to yoga classes twice a week. It occurred to me this undertaking was developing into an unpaid, part-time job and was starting to kill my social life. Apart from Steve and my girlfriend, I'd sometimes go weeks without seeing friends or even straying far from the route between my building and the YMCA.

Though the tides are changing, for decades juggling routines, especially in competition, had followed a fairly predictable model. If someone were to make a bingo card for an evening of juggling competition, it would include squares with:

- Vests
- Some wacky, offbeat object juggled or manipulated
- Props set up randomly around the stage
- Three or more pirouettes in a routine
- Juggling at least five objects for individuals, or passing at least nine objects for teams
- Very briefly juggling (aka "flashing") at least seven objects for individuals, or passing 10 objects for teams
- Rings routine finished by pulling them down around one's neck
- Same tricks that won last year
- Get the audience to clap rhythmically for some stunt
- "Discover" a prop lying on the stage, say a ball, examine it in a "what on earth is this alien thing?" manner for a beat, then begin to manipulate it with increasing skill
- A Top 10 hit from the previous year used as background music (everyone takes a shot if two competitors use the same music)

Steve and I were doing none of this. We were only juggling clubs, there would be no gimmicks, no other props, no numbers passing (i.e. passing seven, eight, nine or 10 objects) and, somewhat daringly, no music.

We had decided way back in the 90s that we were better off talking through our performances. Almost no one did this, but we felt it paired well with our whole stripped down, raw approach to the act. The Nirvana of club passing, if you will.

Also, initially we assumed there would a lots of drops, and picking up repeated drops to music looks awkward. We needed to have prepared "drop lines" ready to go—jokes acknowledging the drop that fill time and entertain as we reset the trick.

Intentionally eschewing a few unspoken, yet effectively fundamental team juggling competition elements like juggling nine or 10 objects was risky, but we felt the overall technical difficulty, creativity and envelope-pushing nature of our six-club passing tricks would deep-fry their brainpans so thoroughly that they'd forget about us flouting any perceived standards.

As any athlete knows, training has its ups and downs. Encouragingly, we made remarkable progress in the first few months.[143] We took every trick and broke it down to the tiniest fractions of movement to see how we might make it

---

[143] If you'd seen us practice before 2013, you'd know "progress" was really the only direction available with most of our tricks.

more consistent. A subtle change in spin, height, speed, timing, grip, even the positioning of a single finger on a club during a throw was making a noticeable difference.

Historically, Steve and I were known as "catchers," meaning we were far better at catching crappy, wild throws than executing, or caring about, throwing accurately. This is why we complemented each other so well. Neither of us gave much thought to our throws, but it didn't matter because we were so good at catching each other's garbage. The downside was this habit was a huge liability whenever Steve and I would pass clubs with someone else, because that person usually expected, even insisted on, accurate throws. Committing a few, if any, misfires toward the face or groin is definitely frowned upon by the vast majority of jugglers. Now, not only did we need to reprogram years of instinct and laziness to become "throwers," but we had to do it quickly, while still being exceptional catchers.

Our practice sessions became downright clinical, dissecting old tricks, sometimes without even juggling and working with just one or two clubs, to refine tiny movements. "OK, so now we know when I kick the club at you with this angle, it smacks you in both kneecaps at the same time. Obviously, that's some ninja shit I'm going to file away for later, but in the meantime how do we keep that from happening in competition?" And so forth.

"Three into Five," which I explained in detail waaaay back, was one of the tricks we drilled the most. It was, and is, both a Duck and Cover signature trick and one of the most difficult tricks we were planning to perform. I don't mean to boast here, but my notable skill for throwing different varieties of three-club multiplexes was already well established. Yet, throwing a three-club multiplex with perfect height, distance and spin for Three into Five to work, over and over, is one of the many juggling-related skills that's essentially a middle finger to the limits of the human body and physics. Hours of drilling were needed to program new methods into my muscle memory to increase our consistency.

If someone were to make a sports movie training montage of us practicing Three into Five, it would mostly be clips of me, wild-eyed and sweating lavishly, getting bent out of shape about making any one of 1,482 minuscule errors with that infernal multiplex throw.

Meanwhile, on Steve's side, even when my three-club multiplexes were perfect, he still had the daunting task of quick-starting a five-club cascade, keeping it going for 6-12 throws, then easing out of it, by making blind passes to me to clear his hands.

We'd never done this degree of repetition or analysis before, because why bother? Flinging clubs around at juggling club and gleefully coping with the anarchy once a week was all the fun we needed. With countless small adjustments we were soon hitting tricks 50-70 percent of the time that we'd formerly only get 10-20 percent of the time. This initial rapid improvement was highly motivating.

Then the plateau began. We made little to no progress for months. The following winter, eight months into training, weeks would go by when, unbelievably, it seemed like we were actually getting worse. I was frustrated. It was my feeling that after eight months of dedicated work, there shouldn't be extended periods where the clubs go spiraling off in new and interesting directions or just helplessly fall from our hands for no reason, something we call "dork drops." It was a good thing that ever-mellow Steve was there to keep me in check, because there were days I would have happily tossed my prop bag into a wood chipper and taken up the harpsichord or some other hobby where errors didn't mean somehow being smacking in the back of the head.[144]

It was about this time, while I was all-consumed with training and peaking frustrations, that my dusty brain meandered to memories of my old hero Scott Burton and his experiences competing in the IJA championships. He didn't medal his first time competing in the senior individuals championship in 1983, however he also competed in the teams championship that year with Bryan Wendling and they won! In 1984, Scott didn't medal in individuals again and he and Bryan went to pieces on stage in the teams championship as they were "plagued with drops," placing 5th.

Scott finally found his groove in 1986 when he won the silver medal. He likely would have won gold, but that

---

[144] That said, if I could make that happen on purpose, it would so be in the show.

was the year fledgling juggling god, Anthony Gatto, blew everyone away in the seniors category at the tender age of 14.[145]

Scott's final appearance on the IJA championship stage was in 1991, where not only did nothing seem to go right for him, but he slid on a dropped ball and fell hard on the stage, obviously injuring himself. He finished the act, but it was not easy to watch.

These memories of Scott's triumphs and, more notably, gut-retching failures gave me pause. If someone as gifted as Scott could have a horrifically bad day on his sixth appearance on the championship stage, was there ever going to be a time when Steve and I—the on fire, almost out of gas, 100 miles from an airport passenger jet of juggling—were confident and consistent enough to even make it through the preliminary auditions?

To make matters worse, we had a significant milestone rushing up: performing in the public show at the Madfest Juggling Festival in Madison, Wisconsin. It would be the first time Steve and I performed on stage together in about 16 years. And boy did it show.

It was the NBA All-Star Game of clubs hitting the floor. This train wreck was partly out of our control. We were only allowed a brief warm up on the stage and then we had to wait more than an hour before our act, sitting in the

---

[145] Gatto had competed three times previously. Once in the juniors category in 1981 (age 9), which he won, then again in 1982 and 1983 (ages 10 and 11) courageously jumping up to the seniors category where he won silver and bronze respectively.

theater's cramped, unheated basement. In Madison, Wisconsin. In January. Though we bundled up and juggled as much as we could in the tiny space, we hit the stage with our hands, arms and shoulders only one step away from being stone cold.

After a respectable period of drinking to forget, we studied the show video obsessively, made some adjustments and managed a strong rebound. We were in top form a month later when we hit the stage for the 2014 MONDO Jugglefest public show. We were so confident that we were planning to submit the video from the show as our prelim audition for the IJA championships that summer.

We made it two-thirds of the way through the act with only a few forgivable drops. Then Steve performed what was possibly the gentlest, yet most painful, show-ending throw in the history of juggling.

For a trick we call "The Balance," what's *supposed* to happen is Steve lightly throws a club with 3/4 of a spin, which I catch in a standing balance on another club in my right hand. However, in this case, the thrown club had a baby's breath more forward momentum than I was prepared for.

It had been nearly two decades since the last time the juggling gods had sabotaged me with the on-stage Leif Curse. And that they'd had so much time to brainstorm and craft creative disasters really showed. The top end of the balance club tipped forward, right into my open eye, knocking out my contact lens. In 20 years of wearing contacts while juggling it was the first time I had lost a lens. Naturally, it had to happen while I was on stage in front of 700 people.

    Amazingly, the lens was stuck to my cheek, not lost forever on the floor. I couldn't see exactly where it was, so Steve picked it off my face and handed it to me. Now take a moment here to consider the frequency that juggling props are dropped. With the amount of time our clubs spend on the ground, our hands end up being effectively covered in floor. Both of us had now touched the lens with hands covered in the collective grime from the bottoms of thousands of pairs of shoes.

    As well equipped with drop lines as Steve and I were, it hadn't occurred to us to have a contingency for occasions when one of us is totally incapacitated on stage for several minutes. A reasonable person in this situation would have said, "Show's over, folks. I'm gonna go burn this contact lens. Good night!" But we are Duck and Cover, perhaps the only juggling team in the world whose popularity can be largely attributed to bad decisions. So, Steve started stalling for time, doing any goofball thing that crossed his mind, while my mind raced trying to figure out what to do next.

    We got no help from the M.C. and stage hands, though to be fair they had probably never seen a club-assisted contact lens removal at a juggling show either, so they weren't bursting with split-second solutions.

    While Steve babbled on, with my back to the audience, I performed the contact lens re-insertion equivalent of a basketball game time-expiring, full-court fling and swish. I got that dry, poop-covered lens back into my eye on stage, with no mirror and my hands shaking with adrenalin. Normally, that task would have been impossible with even one of those impediments.[146]

My eyes were now watery and on fire. The stage manager hurried down the aisle from the lighting/sound booth in the back of the theater, holding up a small bottle of eye drops. She later told me she brings eye drops to every show, because you never know. I still wonder what else she has in her bag. Tourniquets?

The eye drops rescue went so smoothly, people thought we'd planned the whole thing. Unfortunately, they didn't help. I was suffering what was, by far, the worst eye pain and blindness I'd experienced in my life.[147] We somehow got through the final part of the act, but due to the time wasted on my stupid lens we had to skip several tricks, and any chance of submitting the video as our championships audition was crushed.

We ended up submitting an audition video made in the gym at the YMCA, with only four drops, with the camera unmanned on a tripod and an echo so disastrous that many of our hilarious lines were drowned out. Despite this, we were accepted into the competition. Though we soon learned

---

[146] If you'd like to actually see this painful, freak accident, go to YouTube and search "I lose a contact lens on stage at the MONDO Jugglefest."
[147] Not counting the time a mutant bee stung me in the forehead when I was 14 and my eyes swelled shut for two days.

this wasn't necessarily because we had dazzled the prelim judges with our tricks.

In a bizarre twist, only three teams auditioned to compete in 2014. In the interest of not having the shortest, least suspenseful team championships in decades, the championships judges probably didn't have any other choice but to accept all three teams.

Suddenly, our original goal to earn a medal, any medal, was rendered moot. We would get a medal just by showing up and successfully controlling our urethras on stage for eight minutes. Also, while the other teams were good, filled with worthy and experienced competitors, they were not god-like. It dawned on us that if we didn't completely melt down on stage, we could actually win this bastard.

The International Jugglers' Association hosts its annual festival and championships in a different location each year. In 2014, it took place in the Purdue University sports center, where the staff seemingly glean much of their life's joy telling paying guests precisely which square feet of the facility they can and can't stand in.

In addition to that indignity, Purdue is located in West Lafayette, Indiana, a down-and-out, fourth-tier town seemingly abandoned by ATM technicians,[148] where chicken-fried steak is their signature local dish and the tap water

---

[148] I've had easier experiences withdrawing cash in the mountains of Laos.

tastes like botulism. It's not someplace you'd voluntarily spend a week if you didn't absolutely have to.

Steve and I had to suffer through three anxious days before the night of the championships. Since we didn't want to rehearse in front of everyone in the gym, and the crack staff at Purdue had an average response time of less than two minutes each time someone stepped a toe in a no-go room of the building, we were reduced to practicing outside, behind a campus garage for privacy.

I can't speak for Steve, but those three days were heart-racing agony for me. I couldn't enjoy any of the activities or events at the festival and my brain was spinning at 3,000 rpm all night long, which made it challenging to sleep soundly for more than a few hours. In a somewhat delirious attempt to maximize my mental and physical state, I'd resolved to stay dry the final three months before the championships, so having a drink or two to calm nerves was out of the question.

I was operating on pure adrenalin the day of the competitions. The tech rehearsal went extremely well. The stage lights weren't a problem at all (rare for juggling in a theater) and the floor was nice and solid, making our distinctive club bouncing tricks much easier and more responsive than on the softer gym floors we usually practiced on.

In the final minute before we hit the stage, Steve and I experienced a bizarre default emotional swap. Normally unflappable, Steve was clearly nervous and for some reason I wasn't. After months of lying awake and fretting over this moment, and having already burned through a year's worth of adrenalin that day, I became remarkably relaxed. Even as the M.C. introduced us and we strolled on stage, I was strangely calm. It's possible I was too calm.

The majority of competition juggling routines generally follow a slow build-up model. The juggler(s) start with the low-key, easy tricks, which get more and more difficult, and build to the crazy highlights at the end. We were doing a "mix tape" approach. The plan was to start out with a zinger, then while the crowd is on their heels, follow with a few lesser tricks they've never seen before, then bring it up a notch, maintain a high level of amazingness, another zinger, and so on with the ups and downs, ending with a killer trick. Like a mix tape[149] of music you'd make for a friend—if you know what you're doing.

The first trick in our routine is one of our most difficult—a wildly inventive, three-part combination trick called "Not Done Yet." I'll do my best to describe it: Without interrupting the six-club passing pattern or rhythm, I collect two clubs in both my right and left hands, throw the two clubs in my left up and simultaneously bat them both toward Steve using the two clubs in my right. Then I quickly throw the two clubs in my right hand at Steve as a multiplex hatchet throw. Finally, while all that commotion is in the air and being dealt with by Steve, I quickly collect the final two

---

[149] Note about mix tapes for #KidsTheseDays: Ask your parents.

clubs in my right hand, drop them and kick *them* simultaneously at Steve with my right foot.

If all this sounds like unpredictable chaos, you'd be absolutely right. Three very difficult, unpredictable multi-club passes and six mostly improvised catches, all happening in about three seconds. It's the kind of borderline suicidal lunacy that has no business on the championships stage. We hoped it would leave the audience and judges gasping.

Amazingly, with hours of agonizing analysis and training, this is a trick we can land about 80 percent of the time on good days. Alas, on stage that night, in four tries we had four "drop events" (the official judging term) and never landed the trick cleanly. Our mix tape strategy was undone.

Two tricks later, another demoralizing drop event on a trick with a 98.99 percent success rate. We rallied, nailed three tricks in a row, then came the club bouncing tricks.

Almost no one does club bouncing because, well, it's not easy, but it's also incredibly rough on the clubs. People who do club bouncing tricks have to be prepared to break (and buy) a lot of clubs, at about $25 a pop.

While bouncing on the solid stage floor was much more responsive, over the previous 18 months of training we'd become accustomed to softer gym floors. The better stage floor became a liability. Using the same throwing force we'd imprinted in our muscle memory, our bounces became erratic and we weren't adapting well with the clock ticking, under the hot glare of stage lights. We dropped on three consecutive tricks, including a high percentage trick where I bounce a club over to Steve's right foot and he kicks it back up into the pattern, which took us four heartbreaking attempts to land.

While we weren't totally melting down, after 11 mostly avoidable drop events in the first half, we were one knee-buckling shot to the groin away from the kind of failure people talk about in pitying tones for years.

But in the second half, in what was probably a surprise to everyone involved, particularly me and Steve, we got our shit together. In a flurry of some of our most difficult tricks, we only suffered four drop events, two of them of the aforementioned regrettably avoidable "dork drop" variety. Ultimately, with 15 total drop events, about triple what we suffer in an average run-through, our chances for gold were looking grim. Though, I feel compelled to add that the underdog effect, compounded by our original and insane tricks, earned us a partial standing ovation.

Among the team competitors, we'd performed first. Now Steve and I had to not have cardiac infarctions, while we spent the next hour and a half watching the other teams compete, mixed in with individual competitors that were also competing that night. It was like waiting for a slow, chatty person to prepare a four-course meal after surviving a plane crash in the desert, followed by a two-week stagger to civilization.

The next team, unbelievably, had even more drop events than we did. This team had five people, who did a tightly choreographed club passing routine, weaving around each other as they juggled. This arrangement made drops even more pronounced as clubs hit the floor in large numbers, followed by scampering around to get back into positions to pick up their cues.

I had seen them run through their routine several times with only a fraction of the drops, which made their performance all the more painful to watch. I wondered if that's how the audience felt while watching me and Steve. I was also doing the mental math as our chances at gold increased with every fumble.

The third and final team was a duo who did an experimental, concept-heavy routine. This act was tricky to judge, at least for me. Their act was highly unique and much of it was pleasantly visual, but it wasn't especially difficult. This style of juggling is not my cup of tea. I've watched far too many abstract, highfalutin jugglers stray dangerously over the line of self-indulgence and, even with a high difficulty factor, these tiresome components become too distracting to appreciate the routine as a whole.

Presumably with the judging criteria in mind,[150] this team didn't let concept eclipse audience enjoyment, but I nevertheless felt my appreciation for their performance slipping at times. They also had several regrettable drops, though notably fewer than Steve and I. Audience reaction was strong, but not hysterical. I honestly did not know which

---

[150] Stage presence, element of risk, presentation, creativity, difficulty, execution and entertainment.

routine would please the judges more: casual insanity or measured concept.

Finally, after all the acts had competed and the judges had spent an indulgently long time sequestered away, tallying and double checking the scores and, I impatiently speculated, knitting a large sweater, the medals presentation ceremony arrived. Steve and I had conferred after all three teams had competed and he too wasn't certain where we stood. It seemed to us it was very close—virtually a toss-up.

We both sat down in the wings as the presentation begun, Steve radiating nervous energy and me not entirely sure my legs could maintain a standing position.

The bronze medal was presented to the five-man club passing team, no surprise there. As they presented the silver medal, my overloaded brain fighting the urge retreat into a coma, I barely heard the words "Duck and Cover."

Days later, with the benefit of hindsight, I concluded that even with fewer drops it was unlikely we would have won. The gold medalists, who had competed three times before and learned hard lessons from previous experience, had a well-rounded routine that handily satisfied every category of the judging criteria. Not to mention fewer drops. We would have had to do a near perfect routine to threaten their win.

Furthermore, when the scoring breakdown was posted the following day, it was clear that a couple judges had not warmed to our style like the audience had. Our disregard for a few of the unspoken team juggling criteria (namely juggling eight, nine and 10 objects), our "unprofessional" costumes[151] and our laid-back presentation had clearly counted against us. In some cases, we were bafflingly shorted in categories where we should have had '11's, like difficulty, creativity and element of risk. While some scoring dings were expected, particularly with all the drops, it was still a bit of a shock.

The dork drops, which I'll just attribute to nerves, were certainly disappointing, but the thing that haunts me most was never cleanly landing Not Done Yet. In what a more spiritual person might have interpreted as cruel knife-twisting by the universe, the day after the competition, standing in the middle of the main festival gym surrounded by gawkers, we were able to run Not Done Yet six or seven times in a row without a drop, repeatedly.

Will I compete again? A younger and better funded version of me would probably shake it off, buy a bucket of ibuprofen and start preparing for a comeback. But age, time and money are against me.

More importantly, we inspired the next generation of wildly inventive club passers literally overnight. I'm told the day after the competitions, during the Creative Club Passing workshop, a lot of the tricks people were developing and practicing were very clearly inspired by the tricks we'd done in competition.

As in most disciplines, juggling innovation never stands still for long. Younger, faster and more creative

---
[151] T-shirts the same color as our clubs and khaki pants.

people, blessed with far more free time and no mortgage payments, will almost definitely take our tricks, build on them and make them better. I'm comfortable with the idea of stepping back from the cutting edge, leaning back in a chair with a cold drink and watching what we started go to previously unimaginable new heights.

We'll keep hatching crazy new tricks, of course. The second best juggling team in the world has a certain reputation to uphold.

Juggling, My Old Friend

"The Bigger, Harder Finish" – Duration: 5.8 seconds

This trick was designed after we decided "The Big Finish" was too easy. In the Big Finish, Steve collects two clubs in his right hand and gives them a static push-throw to my right hand, so I can catch them both simultaneously. He does this again, throwing the next pair of clubs to my left hand. Now I'm holding four of the six clubs in the pattern. Steve collects the final two clubs in his right hand and throws a two-club multiplex hatchet throw to me, which I scissors catch, one in each hand. With me holding all six clubs in a hard stop of the juggling, this seemed like a good trick to end our act.

Now, the Bigger, Harder Finish is the same, except Steve throws a two-club multiplex end-bounce off the floor toward me, which I scissors catch.

As you can plainly see and understand by this stage in the book, the first way is *way* too easy, controlled and predictable to be worthy of inclusion a Duck and Cover routine.

Apart from my family and my oldest friend, juggling has been the longest continual presence in my life. Like any long-term relationship, we've had some ups and downs.

The passion was fast and furious in the beginning, because I had never juggled before, but I'd heard so much about it and I didn't want to be the last one among my friends to juggle, but then I finally juggled and it was amazing and I just wanted to juggle all the time, like at the park, between classes at school, under the bleachers and even in my bedroom when my parents weren't home. Ah, young juggling.

The passion subsided and after a period of coasting along in an agreeably neutral state, I became distracted and left juggling to sow my oats elsewhere, only to discover that juggling was the best thing out there all along. My half-hearted relationship with high school wrestling, for example, is something I could have lived without. I experimented outside of juggling again in college and was romanced long enough to actually get a degree in theater arts. But that too eventually ended in a messy divorce.[152] Eventually, juggling and I got back together.

During both high school and college, I distinguished myself as someone who attended every minute of class, but still somehow didn't perform well.[153] I'm probably indebted to juggling for at least some compensation, via my memory, concentration, and applied logic. Indeed, these strengths, in addition to problem anticipation, identification and

---

[152] One can only take so much rejection and starvation income before the grass looks irresistibly greener over in Juggleville.
[153] You'll recall that late in my college years, this mystery was seemingly solved by identifying my delightful mix of dyslexia and achingly slow, indecipherable handwriting.

avoidance, are likely a major factor in how I've been able to navigate 57 countries with hardly a lick of trouble.

In my early 30s, a work opportunity split us up, this time for more than four years, while I gallivanted around the planet, pursuing my travel writing dreams. Those years were so hectic, I didn't really miss juggling. Well, not actively. That much time away from juggling had a noticeable effect on my overall mental and physical state, however. It finally occurred to me that my connection to juggling went far deeper than a normal relationship. We had become almost symbiotic. I needed juggling to be the best version of me.

As soon as my lifestyle allowed for it, I reunited with juggling and today we're as close as ever. I'm not quite fanatical enough to make juggling the center of my identity, attending a dozen festivals a year[154] or walking around wearing T-shirts that say things like "I just had a healthy ball movement."[155] But it's certainly among my top life priorities.

It's my primary form of both physical and mental exercise. I travel for, and spend a fair amount of money on, juggling. I obviously compare a lot of things in everyday life to juggling, like the unforgivable lameness of baseball.

It's also been an emotional standby throughout some of the roughest parts of my life. When I went through a downturn of social popularity in junior high school,[156]

---

[154] Like Steve.
[155] This isn't a real T-shirt, but it should be.
[156] Which began in late grade school, but those were mostly pre-juggling years.

juggling and juggling club were reliable fallbacks, in addition to being a confidence-builder that would pay off later in life.

During the brutal two years of my glacial divorce, apart from a few treasured friends and some powerful antidepressants, juggling was my crutch.

Having worked from home for the bulk of the past 15 years, there have been days that juggling was the only reason I left my condo. And as recently as early 2018, juggling helped me recover from back-to-back surgeries, when things like biking or weightlifting were completely out of the question.

If not for juggling, I might have found other anchors that filled all these needs. I might have had [dry heave] kids. Or followed in my father's footsteps and become an amateur bike racer, with a nice collection of road rash scars and concussions to prove it.

On the other hand, particularly in light of my escalating introversion over the past decade, I might have just as easily become a hopeless shut-in, spending all my free time playing video games and writing outraged opinion pieces about all the screw-ups in the latest comic book film adaptation.[157]

Having juggling as a hobby has led to many funny, interesting, bizarre, and offensive moments over the years. When any activity or sport is such a key component in your life, it doesn't take long for it to come out while speaking to

---

[157] Yes, I'm aware that writing a lengthy juggling memoir isn't far removed from that spot on the Geek Assessment chart.

new friends and coworkers, doctors, masseurs, at parties, and at the bus stop when someone inquires about what the hell you have in the huge bag with odd protrusions on the sides.

No bowl of fruit is safe at any party after I've been outed as a juggler.

I'm happy to report that, even in the lean years of the 1980s and 90s, when juggling was little more than a popular punch line, most people have regarded my lifestyle as a positive, if not an intriguing curiosity. Common follow-up questions include:

- "Do you juggle fire and knives and stuff?"
- "Are you in the circus? You should try out for the circus!"
- "What is the most things you've ever juggled?"
- "My brother/cousin/neighbor/college roommate can juggle oranges."
- "I could never learn how to juggle."
- "I went to Cirque du Soleil once."

Being "that guy that juggles" can be a drag, too. It's prone to abuse, like people calling their doctor and lawyer friends for free advice. It's frequently made me the go-to guy for friends and coworkers when some form of cheap/free entertainment is required at an off-hours personal or work function.

Juggling has also played a part in my travels over the years. In addition to my efforts at performing on the street, I sometimes showed up unannounced at local juggling clubs around the world, just to meet a few locals (and use their props for a little practice).

What I'm getting at, in addition to all the aspects I described throughout this book, is that juggling appears to play a larger role in everyday life than most hobbies. It's a defining feature of one's overall identity, like pro athlete, politician or travel writer.[158] I've known it was awesome since the beginning, but, simpletons like Jackasselhoff and Piers Morgan aside, juggling commands an advanced degree of respect and dignity that I didn't quite grasp for a long time.[159] This applies to everyone from Renaissance Festival clowns to the current and future Gattos of the world.

Even after 35 years, juggling is awe-inspiring and sexy. It's beautiful and badass, technical and comical, fresh and surprising. But most importantly, it's like an old friend. Even if you don't see each other for years, within minutes of being reunited you fall right back into a familiar comfort zone and banter.[160]

Assuming no calamities, Steve-assisted or otherwise, no matter what undreamt of turns society takes or traumas our ailing planet endures, I'm looking forward to another 35 years of juggling. It's just out there, hovering over me, invisible but always present. It's instantly available with little preparation, like running or sleeping. It's a component of my being that shapes and affects a rather amazing amount of my existence, even when juggling props are nowhere in sight.

Most important of all, it's fun. Unlike baseball, which I hate.

---

[158] I couldn't resist.
[159] To be fair, I wasn't grasping much of anything subtle until I was, like, 24.
[160] Except for particularly complex things, like juggling seven balls. I can assure you that if you stop practicing that, then try to pick it up again 15 years later, this particular friend has no effing idea who you are and would really rather not hang out.

Author Biography

Leif Pettersen is a freelance writer, humorist, insatiable traveler, and world class juggler from Minneapolis, Minnesota.

Pettersen's first book is *Backpacking with Dracula: On the Trail of Vlad "the Impaler" Dracula and the Vampire He Inspired.* Part travel memoir and part historical profile of 15th-century Prince Vlad Dracula III, the book explores fact, legend and fiction about Vlad and confusion with Bram Stoker's Dracula, while traveling through modern Romania.

Pettersen has authored Lonely Planet guidebooks for Romania, Tuscany and Moldova, and has been a prolific contributor to LonelyPlanet.com. His work has appeared in Global Traveler magazine, MSN, USA Today, the Minneapolis Star Tribune, Minnesota Monthly, San Francisco Chronicle, BBC Travel, CNN Travel, Cara (Aer Lingus in-flight magazine), SkyLife (Turkish Airlines magazine), Skift, vita.mn, The Growler, and Juggle magazine.

Pettersen loves chocolate, hates pickles, types with exactly four fingers, and can escape from a straitjacket. In 2014, he won a silver medal at the world juggling championships as one half of the duo Duck and Cover. He has not vomited since 1993, making him a consummate travel journalist and excellent party guest.

leifpettersen.com

@leifpettersen

Made in the USA
Coppell, TX
13 December 2019